S0-AFX-482

# Peace Theory

## Preconditions
### *of* Disarmament

# Peace Theory

PRECONDITIONS *of* DISARMAMENT

BY

# John·W·Burton

ALFRED·A·KNOPF : NEW YORK

1962

L. C. catalog card number: 62–15951

THIS IS A BORZOI BOOK,

PUBLISHED BY ALFRED A. KNOPF, INC.

Copyright © 1962 by John W. Burton. All rights
reserved. No part of this book may be reproduced in
any form without permission in writing from the
publisher, except by a reviewer, who may quote brief
passages in a review to be printed in a magazine or
newspaper. Manufactured in the United States of
America, and distributed by Random House, Inc.
Published simultaneously in Toronto, Canada, by
Random House of Canada, Limited.

FIRST EDITION

# Preface

International Affairs is not a discipline. As a term it describes an extensive field of inquiry including the study of peaceful relations among nations. This more limited field *could* be a discipline. However, the thinking of the earlier philosophers and the more recent work of political scientists have not been brought together into any system which assists in solving the problems of international relations. There has been a good deal of discussion as to the desirability of doing this, but as yet no discipline has emerged.

Unless the political scientist can draw a precise pattern of a stable condition of peace, unless there can be presented to the politician a picture of a disarmed world in which there will be no tendencies toward rearmament, any achievement of peaceful international relationships will be largely accidental.

The present work is an attempt to provide some basic theory for those concerned with the formulation of policy. If it fails to do so, a second aim is to demonstrate that such a guide is possible, and that more work along these lines would be fruitful.

The first two chapters state the problem. Importance is attached to these, for without a history of the case and a description of the symptoms, diagnosis and treatment are likely to be in error. The next five chapters are concerned with theory. In Chapter Seven the analysis is translated into policy terms. There follow some comments on the difference between a scientific and a pragmatic approach to the formulation of policy, and some observations as to the point of political responsibility to which studies of this nature have ultimately to be directed.

Any fresh treatment of a subject inevitably raises side issues, especially in relation to study and to teaching. To round off consideration of theory and its application, some of these issues are dealt with in the final chapter.

The title *Peace Theory* has been given to this work, for that is what it is in methodological terms. It is, consequentially, also an analysis of policies which would be required in a disarmed world by nations wishing to avoid provocations leading to rearmament. It has, therefore, both a theoretical and a practical aspect, which explains the subtitle, *Preconditions of Disarmament*.

JOHN W. BURTON

*Australian National University*
*May, 1961*

# Acknowledgments

This book was written while I was a Visiting Fellow to the Australian National University in the School of Pacific Studies. My thanks are due, therefore, to those who made possible the fellowship, and more especially to those who helped with suggestion and criticism. Professor, Sir John Crawford, the Director of the School, Professor P. H. Partridge, whose field is Social Philosophy, Mr. R. S. Parker, working in Political Science, and Mr. A. L. Burns, whose special interests are in international relations, were most generous with their time. Dr. Appadorai of the School of International Studies at New Delhi, and the members of the Pugwash Group which met in Moscow in 1960, were among those whose stimulating observations helped in the preparation of this book.

J. W. B.

# Contents

Contents

Contents

# Peace Theory

## Preconditions
### *of* Disarmament

# I

## The Problem Stated:
## Forms of Conflict

### 1. THE NATURE OF INTERNATIONAL RELATIONS

International life is inevitably a dynamic condition of unrelenting competition among nations for trade and commerce, for prestige and status, and for the winning of allegiances and the promotion of ideologies. Deliberate attempts to outmaneuver and to defeat in constant battle for position, prestige, and power are a normal feature of relations among states. A condition of stable peaceful relations is not likely to be an undisturbed day-by-day international relationship, nor one in which there is general acceptance of any existing international structure. Competition, even in a theoretically perfect condition of peaceful relationships, would tend to be pushed at least to the limits beyond which peace would be destroyed. Such aggressive competition follows automatically from the existence of independent and sovereign states.

3

The study of peaceful international relations does not seek to eliminate this competition. It seeks rather to prevent conflict from being resolved by warfare, that is, to make unnecessary the employment of warfare as an instrument of national policy. It seeks, furthermore, to ensure that conflict is resolved and not merely repressed; for the repression of conflict merely suppresses grievances, and unsatisfied grievances create a condition not of peace but of potential hostility. The study of peaceful international relations is concerned, therefore, with the regulation of competitive rivalries in international relations in such a way as to secure for each nation the greatest possible satisfactions from competition without recourse to war.

The organization and controls which seem to be required to prevent warfare in one circumstance and in one age may not be appropriate in another. The maintenance of peaceful international relations may seem to demand one system in an age of geographic discovery and of competition for new markets, another in an age of rapid industrial development, and yet another in a nuclear age. The forms and structures of international organization should be relevant to the nature of the competition which they are required to regulate. Conflict could be aggravated by an international structure which might have been considered relevant in one stage but which is not appropriate to another. Tribal warfare may once have been an important and even a valuable social institution; but it ceased to be useful. The "balance of power" may have been an effective means of maintaining stability while at the same time permitting periodic change and new balances in a period of expansion, discovery, and invention; but it could be irrelevant in an age of ideological competition, and disastrous in a nuclear age.

4

Moreover, organization and controls in international relations must accord with the political thinking and the social values of the day. Interstate war was in classical times commonly held to be an acceptable and, in the view of many, a natural institution. Material damage and loss of life were not great. As the nature of warfare altered, there developed new values, and warfare as such was universally condemned.

The nuclear weapon made war as an instrument of national policy not merely undesirable, but also impracticable. Yet competition and conflict remained a feature of international life. Inasmuch as war was impracticable as the ultimate means of resolving conflict, new processes and new structures for international organization were required.

Unless the nature of competition and of conflict, that is, the nature of the problem to be solved, is reassessed and restated as conditions alter, inherited structures and policies are likely to be retained which have no relevance to the circumstances where they are being applied, and which may in practice defeat their own objectives. There are reasons for thinking, as will be argued, that the national policies and international structures of the twentieth century, inherited from past ages, are not appropriate to the circumstances with which they are required to deal.

## 2. FORMS OF CONFLICT

As Carr observed[1] in reference to the causes of World War II, the most aggressive and most frequent form of competition between sovereign states is between the dynamic and the static. The attack on existing structure by the

1 Carr, E. H.: *Conditions of Peace* (London: The Macmillan Co.; 1944).

5

state undergoing change or desirous of bringing change about is stimulated by a variety of circumstances arising out of economic, social, and political changes of all kinds which are taking place continuously in the international environment.

### i: Classical Conflict

Dispute over boundaries, claims to newly discovered territories, rivalry for the possession of colonial territories, and disagreement over rights to exploitation were among the most common forms of conflict until the twentieth century. In the view of the conservative power, justice was equated with law—law of possession and law of agreement; but in the view of the revolutionary power, the existing situation was unjust and had to be changed by force if necessary. There was little compromise possible between the two positions. Resort to force either maintained the existing position or altered it. A modern example of this type of classical conflict was the attempt in 1956 by Britain and France to maintain their interests when Egypt set out to nationalize the Suez Canal. They adopted a legal view based on agreements, and the revolutionary power adopted a different legal view based on its rights of sovereignty. The dispute between the Dutch and Indonesian Governments in the fifties and sixties over the possession of the Western section of New Guinea had some of these classical characteristics. The territory under dispute was one of the few "no-man's lands" left, one of the few remaining areas of the world still in an underdeveloped and dependent state. Neither party had claims other than legal ones based on agreements and past structures about which there was no agreed interpretation. The

6

peoples of the island were not in a position to press claims for independence.

Border disputes were among the earliest form of conflict. After the Second World War there remained a number, largely as a result of decisions made during the war. The division of Korea and of Germany, in particular, created artificial boundaries about which the peoples concerned were not consulted. Border disputes are likely to be a source of conflict until all boundaries are established and recognized in relation to the sovereignty of the governments concerned. Independence of sovereign governments is not the only requirement. Border disputes arising out of ideological and other competition for the allegiance of small nations are likely to occur at least until independent sovereign states are well established and widely supported by their own peoples. Otherwise, local rebellions, in which the main powers are likely to intervene in their own interests, will tend to divide peoples and to create new or altered borders, at least temporarily. Even though relatively unimportant, such rebellions could be a major source of international conflict between major powers.

Once the discovery of the world was complete, and sovereignty established, one common basis of conflict was virtually removed. The inclusion of the principles of self-determination in the Charter of the United Nations in 1945, and the practical application of this principle during the forties and fifties to most dependent areas in Asia, Africa, and the Middle East, set a course leading to the early and secure independence of peoples, even of peoples who had no means of self-protection against foreign assault. As independent nations are progressively established

7

everywhere and their sovereignty observed, as sovereign rights come to be exercised in place of former rights of exploitation by foreign interests, this classical form of conflict will become less and less important as a source of international dispute.

## ii: Revolt Against Suppression

Revolt against suppression has been another common source of conflict. Suppression has most frequently been inflicted upon peoples occupying an important strategic position, or upon a country possessing strategic resources. Suppression is usually the lot of subject peoples; but there are also independent nations which consider themselves prejudiced by restraints imposed upon their activities by other nations.

World War II in particular offers some support for this view. In the period prior to 1939 revolt was to a large degree the result of conditions arising out of the peace treaties of World War I and out of the Great Depression of the thirties. It was a revolt against tariffs, invisible tariffs (such as health regulations), quotas, economic blocs, subsidies, the discouragement of invention and innovation, controls by industries of their own markets with government support, and other such devices designed to protect the "haves" against the "have nots." Those academic writings of the period which dealt with political tension were concerned largely with discussion of these devices, their causes, and their political effects.

After the early nineteen-thirties, most trading nations imposed restrictions against Japan as part of their own depression policies and in an attempt to meet growing Japanese competition. Japan persisted over a long period in her endeavors to obtain materials and markets, and it was

8

only after it had become clear that there would be no relaxation of discriminatory controls that Japan introduced an exchange permit system in 1937. Subsequent failure by market methods to persuade the rest of the world to allow her to develop led Japan to pursue a policy of securing markets by the bargaining power of force. No passive adjustment to the discriminatory treatment was possible. The Co-prosperity Sphere, a sufficient area to provide raw materials and markets under her own political control, had to be obtained by one means or another if Japanese living standards were to improve.

Consequent developments included the rise to power of those leaders prepared to force the issue. The balance of power was soon altered. It was, however, not the change in balance of power which was the cause of the instability. What caused the war was the treatment of Japan by other powers which, because of their own circumstances, were not prepared to make the adjustments necessary to allow Japan to develop. Similar accounts could be given in relation to Germany and to Italy. In each case the increased military might and the consequent unbalance in power which led finally to war had their origins primarily in economic and related conditions imposed upon these countries by others. In each case there was revolt against suppression.

### iii: Revolt Against Poverty

Poor living conditions and underdevelopment are not necessarily due to current foreign restraints; there are in most cases reasons relating to history and to natural resources. Nevertheless, such conditions are not passively accepted, especially as the peoples concerned become aware of the higher income of others and the means by

9

which their own incomes might be increased. Revolt is likely to be directed against the former colonial power, or against the feudal lord through whom the colonial power operated and to whom the condition of poverty is attributed. The demand for independence can arise out of a belief that independence is in itself a remedy for low living standards. If, as is frequently the case, independence does not quickly produce improved living conditions, the political and economic system inherited from the colonial power may be challenged. Revolt, and if necessary armed revolt, is inevitable in the absence of acceptable minimum living standards. In retrospect, Germany, Italy, and Japan would have required in the thirties economic and technical aid on a large scale (in addition to the removal of discrimination against their goods and of other barriers to their development) before revolt could have been overcome and a condition of peaceful relations established.

The problems of underdevelopment were recognized in the forties, and extensive assistance programs were launched. However, the introduction of economic and technical assistance on a far greater scale yet would have been required in the years after the Second World War in order to establish a condition of acceptable living standards, and to prevent revolts against the international structure.

### iv: Revolt Stimulated by Unaccustomed Hardship

One related special case should be noted, though it is an unusual one. This is the case of an economy, even one with a relatively high living standard, which is dependent on the production of only one or, at most, of a few products, and which cannot shift production to others.

Such an economy is exposed to changed market conditions. Assume the product, say textiles, can be produced in almost every other country as a result of the invention of synthetics, and that for domestic reasons every country decides to protect its own industry. The dependent country is then faced with a market condition which sharply reduces its income. Such a case can arise even after a country has obtained a relatively high living standard and has become accustomed to it. The country would not be willing passively to accept a lower living standard as a result of protective tariffs imposed by other countries against its main product. In the absence of accommodation by others, it would try to obtain under its own political control sufficient areas of raw materials and markets to enable it to maintain its living standard. Usually in the world economy there are sufficient markets and sufficient diversity of national production to prevent this situation. This was not the case, however, before the war when Japan had virtually only one export product, and when world markets were virtually closed to it. The same situation could occur in any developing country dependent wholly, for instance, on rubber or some such product the demand for which suddenly ceased because of substitute products.

*v: Ideological Conflict*

The revolt which led to World War II, a conflict described at the time as being between the "haves" and the "have nots," was not so much a revolution with a philosophy or a developed ideology as a revolution with a particular and immediately practical purpose. Germany, Italy, and Japan set out to overcome particular and immediate problems in their economic life. Revolts against subjection and against poverty were also of this character. By contrast, in the forties and fifties the Communist revolt against the established world order was primarily an ideological one. It did not seek to remedy any specific and immediate international situation of direct concern to the Soviet. It sought to consolidate within its own territories certain ideas and institutions. It sought also, as part of its own consolidation, to promote these ideas and institutions elsewhere. A body of theory and thinking distinguished it from the revolts of Fascism and Nazism, which were systems constructed on the basis of immediate expediency.

Professor R. M. Crawford, one of the contributors to *Paths to Peace*,[2] discounts the part played by ideology in the main periods of history. In his view, ideology was often present, but not as a cause of conflict. In the period 1494-1648, for example, the Age of Reformation, there were indeed strong religious and ideological differences which at times seemed to overshadow all other aspects. In the period of the French Revolution and Napoleon, 1793-1815, the political rather than the religious considerations were all-important. Economic influences seem to have been more important during the first half of the twentieth century, despite the fact that "freedom from tyranny" was the popular theme. Professor Crawford argues, however, that these ideological conflicts were merely a part of cumulative processes. In referring to the period between World War I and World War II, he observes:

> The close relationship of ideological conflicts with these changes needs no elaboration here; it will be enough to instance the spread of Communism dur-

[2] Wallace, V. H., ed. (Melbourne: Melbourne University Press; 1957).

ing the world depression; the relation of Nazism in Germany with the defeat of 1918, the inflation of 1923 and the depression beginning in 1929; and the strength given to Communism in Italy and France by heavy unemployment in the former, and financial and political instability in the latter. . . . In short, this sketch of the role of ideological conflict in international relations suggests that we may easily overestimate its importance, and in doing so overlook deeper causes of war. . . . In time of war, they [ideologies] have provided a political weapon of war, and they have made compromise short of war more difficult to achieve.

In this same book, the Prime Minister of India summarises:

The conclusion is that the view that conflict between opposing ideologies is the main source of international conflict is not supported by historic evidence. . . . The conviction that the present world division is due to ideological conflict justifies, in the minds of those holding such a belief, the propaganda in this regard, and also justifies psychological warfare, fear and suspicion, as the normal mechanism of international behaviour. The ideological aspect today, however, is more the instrument than the cause of our divided world.

This view, which reasonably seeks to set aside emotional responses to new ideological thinking, does not take fully into account the direct effect which Communist ideology as such has had on international relations, first through the techniques of production which the ideology makes possible, and secondly, through its influence on other peoples and nations.

Dramatic industrial development took place in Communist countries, especially in the Soviet. This was first evidenced by military achievement in the nuclear field. By the fifties the Western powers acknowledged this growth and no longer held to the belief that only the incentives of private enterprise could lead to rapid industrial development. The industrial and military potential of communism soon began to overshadow the ideological differences which seemed to be the original source of rivalry. In 1956 one observer commented:

> It has often been pointed out, and quite rightly, that if the Soviet Union were to disappear or have a complete and convincing change of heart with respect to world domination, we should still have to face and solve many problems which we now consider to be aspects of the Soviet threat. . . . We cannot say what would have been the extent or nature of the Russian power challenge to the United States in the absence of Communism, but it is not unreasonable to suppose that there would have been a challenge, based on Russia's new industrial stature.[3]

It would be a mistake, however, to regard this potential as not being causally related to the ideology itself. The incentives and the economic and social organization which rested greatly upon the activities of teachers and organizers scattered throughout the economy, the motivations, the priorities, all developed out of an ideological

[3] Roberts, H. L.: *Russia and America: Dangers and Prospects*, Council on Foreign Relations (New York: Harper & Bros.; 1956), pp. xi, 31.

14

background without which the industrial advances would not have taken place.

Secondly, the political and economic institutions of communism were demonstrated as having a practical relevance to the backward peoples of the world. So much was this the case that it was difficult to determine the relative extent of the influence of the revolutionary power on other peoples, on the one hand, and the indigenous manifestations of the same revolution on the other. The revolt spread far beyond the territories of the revolutionaries. The rapidly growing economic potential and the successful methods of organizing politically backward peoples had, quite inevitably, and quite apart from any aggressive intent that might have been present, a direct bearing on relations with underdeveloped countries. Here again, the ideology was the causal factor without which the political and economic institutions would not have developed, and without which little impact would have been made upon other countries. Soviet leaders certainly related ideology and achievement, and anticipated the spread of the ideology by reason of its achievement. Moscow's *International Affairs* reported:

A revolutionary way of overcoming the economic backwardness of the Eastern countries—this is what the American and other monopolies fear most of all. They advise the underdeveloped countries to wait another century until they, with the "help" of the West, will be able to enjoy the fruits of economic advance. But the peoples of these countries do not want to wait.[4]

[4] *International Affairs*, A Monthly Journal of Political Analysis (Moscow: Jan., 1959), p. 34.

The West seemed to agree with this view, for it was often reflected in United States Congressional Hearings:

> . . . the less developed countries will not wait; they want their economic revolution now, and they expect its fruits within two generations rather than two centuries . . . The advanced industrial nations, already under a cloud on account of their accumulated wealth, are alternately suspected of neglect and of ulterior motives. Russia by contrast postures as a new comer who pulled himself up by his own boot-straps and who is therefore capable of the best disinterested advice.[5]

So true is this today that the typical form of international conflict in the second half of the twentieth century consists of rivalry over the underdeveloped areas. Most of the latter were previously within the Western sphere of influence, but some are being attracted by communism as a means of solving their pressing economic problems. Relations between the Great Powers are governed by their own relative military and political strengths in the particular regions concerned. In some cases military bases have been established by one of the rival powers; in others, regional military pacts have been negotiated under the control of some one power which has sought to defend a particular region from the competitive aggression of another. The weapons of aggression and of defense are military and economic aid, propaganda and espionage, and other techniques of subversion and disruption. It is

[5] *Hearings from the Sub-Committee on Foreign Economic Planning of Joint Economic Committee.* Eighty-fourth Congress, Second Session (Washington: 1957), pp. 60-2.

16

in these relationships that competition between the major powers is most dangerous.

The underdeveloped countries concerned have for the most part been nonaligned in this struggle between the Great Powers. This originally meant little more than that they were preoccupied with their own pressing problems of maintaining life, and that as newly independent countries they considered themselves outside Great-Power conflict. Some have had, and continue to have, historic ties with one power group; some have reacted against these historic ties and favored another. There have been divided loyalties. The common sentiment has been for independence and anticolonialism of all kinds. At a conference of Asian and African states held at Bandung, Indonesia, in 1956, this common interest was made clear both to the West and to the Communist governments. Until this time nonalignment had been regarded by some Western leaders as "immoral," and by the Communist powers, especially China, as at best confused thinking and at worst hidden treachery. As a result of Indian leadership, however, later assisted by Indonesia, and as a result of Asian traditions and philosophy and of the direct contacts made at Bandung by Chinese leaders with Asian leaders, nonalignment survived attacks made upon it and in due course came to be a policy tolerated by both power blocs.

The growth of nonalignment, especially after the creation of many new African states in 1960, changed the character of Great-Power rivalry. By 1960 the "neutrals," as the nonaligned countries were then called, received recognition as a third group of nations when the Soviet suggested a tripartite office of Secretary-General of the

United Nations, comprising nominees of the two power blocs and the neutrals. The nonaligned nations then were at the highest peak of their unity and co-operation.

Their influence did not rest upon their organization as a bloc; in fact they were not so organized. Their common activities and policies were based upon their newly won freedom and independence. This alone did not prove a firm foundation for unity and co-operation except in relation to a limited number of matters concerning colonialism and independence. Their strength was rather in the fact that the nonalignment of the new nations suited the current requirements of the Great Powers. The nuclear stalemate made it expedient for the Great Powers to seek compromise solutions in conflicts taking place in areas in which their competition was most dangerous. In early 1961 the creation of a "neutral" government in Laos seemed to be the solution of an internal conflict favored by both power groups. This reflected a changed attitude on both sides, an acceptance of middle-of-the-road governments, instead of support for extremes favoring one power or another.

A compromise of this nature is a compromise between two ideologies rather than a compromise between two competing industrial systems. The evidence of this ideological conflict was thus to be found in the underdeveloped areas, the uncommitted countries. They provided the arena.

From the point of view of the West, the problem presented by ideological conflict has been far more difficult than the mere resistance of aggression, or the protection of trading and other traditional interests. It has been a problem far greater than the preservation of a status quo. The concept of the status quo was developed with reference to boundaries and to the balance of forces and of power, to conditions which could be maintained by threat of force or reinstated by peace treaties. The threat to the status quo before World War II was a revolutionary movement which was primarily a military one. The conflict was resolved by war, and some approximation to the previous condition resulted from the victory. In the communist-capitalist rivalry, the threat to the status quo arose not out of military strength primarily but out of a dramatic change in relative economic and population strengths of the revolutionary group. The concept of a status quo is meaningless when applied to such a situation. There appears no conceivable way of restoring it short of the deliberate and cold-blooded destruction of at least two major economies comprising nearly one third of the world's population.

The Communist governments have been and are aware of this, and their fears of counterrevolution have been enhanced by many Western statements made at a time when Russia was at a military disadvantage and had no means by which to deter a massive nuclear attack. They have considered that it is they who are maintaining the status quo, and that the danger of war is, for this reason, from the West. An editorial in *International Affairs* (Moscow) dwelt on this, and the high degree of defensive reaction or fear is of interest.

> The interests of world peace make it imperative to accept the fact that in the situation which has taken shape in the world there are capitalist and socialist states. Any attempt to change this situation by outside force, to violate the status quo, and any attempts to precipitate territorial changes would have disas-

trous consequences. What they [the West] are trying to do is to give the present, contemporary status quo a diametrically different interpretation, to reduce it to an entirely different formula, to the formula of status-quo-ante-bellum, i.e., the status which existed before the war and has passed away never to return. It is a trick which is not going to fool anyone. To recognize the present status quo is to accept the changes that have occurred and to accept the present situation as an objective reality which cannot be wiped off the slate either by force of arms or false propaganda.[6]

In practice, the West accepted the new "status quo" —the Soviet interpretation. For this reason it was content to try to "contain" the revolutionary movement. Regional pacts and guarantees to dependent peoples, support for anti-Communist and, very frequently, unpopular feudal regimes, were some of the devices employed. They were ineffective, however, because they did not take into account the strength of the indigenous revolutionary movements in areas outside the contained Communist areas. Demands throughout Asia, Southeast Asia, Africa, and the Middle East for independence and for freedom from internal feudal rule, which had their origins long before China became a Communist state, could not be met by containment. The threat made by the President of the United States in January, 1954, to use "overwhelming" force at a time and place of America's choosing as a means of counteracting local aggression, provided real grounds for a belief among Soviet leaders that the West did not accept the new world order. The Soviet fears re-

[6] Op. cit. (Jan., 1958), pp. 72-5.

mained until their own industrial and scientific development provided weapons which countered the ultimate threat on which containment was based.

Western policy then changed to meet the new situation, and "limited wars" and "controlled armaments" became the basic strategy. This seemed to suggest a far greater acceptance of communism as a permanent state, and to remove some of the Soviet fears of counterrevolution against communism as such by the use of weapons of mass destruction.

The ideological conflict between communism and capitalism has been limited from the outset. The two competing systems have a relevance in time and place which make them applicable only to certain areas and peoples. There are countries in which communism could have little appeal, for instance in the developed economies of the West, and others in which Communist planning and techniques have had an immediate appeal as a means of alleviating economic distress. The competition has been further limited by sentiments of nationalism and independence prevailing among smaller nations, underestimated by both power groups. The preservation of independence is to newly independent states as important a national aim as much needed immediate material gain. "Neutralism" has prevented the strategic alignments which both sides would have considered necessary for successful military conflict.

These limitations, however, were not in the first instance acknowledged by either side, and they have not, therefore, lessened the conflict. On the contrary, attempts by both sides to subjugate countries and to impose their political institutions have been a constant source of conflict between the major powers. The defense of "legitimate" governments is a principle generally accepted, and one of which the rival powers have taken full advantage when it has suited their strategic interests.

Thus the following position emerged. The Communist countries have resented and felt frustrated by attempts to "contain" them, and have feared attempts by the West to destroy their industrial potential as the one means possible to restore a Western "status quo"; the West has feared the consequences of creeping aggression to which there seems no answer; and both see victory over the other in the future of underdeveloped countries which have every wish to benefit from the competition but no wish to be fought over. The nonalignment of Asian countries and the fear of nuclear warfare provide a breathing space in which both power groups have had opportunities to readjust their attitudes and policies. The conflict was in origin and has remained in essence an ideological one, industrial competition being merely one test of ideological superiority.

### vi: Unwarranted Revolt

Some attacks on the existing structure might be thought unwarranted at the time, and also in retrospect. While the possibility of potential conflict of this type has to be considered, the likelihood of its occurrence in a form which would provoke war has to be demonstrated. Most attempts to change existing conditions are regarded as unwarranted and undesirable from some point of view. An argument can usually be produced to condemn change. There are, on the other hand, probably few changes initiated which would so universally be regarded as undesirable, and so completely devoid of justice, as to be termed unwarranted. For instance, changes preceding World War

II were undesirable from the point of view of the Western powers; but they were in a large measure a reaction by Germany and Japan to the refusal of the West to make the necessary adjustments once an economic injustice had been demonstrated. Such situations probably form the great majority of "unwarranted" changes in history. Popular thinking on this issue is confused by misleading analogies. Within the nation state there are murderers and thieves, and provision must be made for their control. Likewise, it is alleged, control is necessary in the international society. Even though the analogy between national and international society could be sustained, the view is still nevertheless a false one. In the state, the law breaker is either *diseased* or is the *maladjusted product of his environment.* The disease concept is not applicable to a nation, however, and so an environmental frustration would have to be, on this analogy, the causal factor of international law breaking. In apparently irresponsible attacks on the status quo, there are probably revolutionary and justice-seeking motivations to be found; and where frustration exists, undesirable, fatal, and self-destructive actions can follow. But such aggressiveness derives from some situation which should have been avoided. The remedy is not, therefore, enforcement or repression; the remedy is, rather, the proper recognition of just claims at a stage early enough to prevent the kind of cumulative political situation in which not even just proposals are likely to receive favorable response. Rigid enforcement of the status quo is bound to create conflict which can be resolved only by force. Recognition on the part of those in power of the perception of injustice on the part of those in revolt is necessary for the avoidance of conflict.

## vii: Irresponsible Action

Closely connected with unwarranted revolt is action by or against "irresponsible" persons—that is, persons, corporations, and powerful interests which have no constitutional policy responsibilities.[7] Foreign capital investment and international monopolies and cartels can create frustrations and resentments. The "irresponsible" acts of private commercial organizations can frequently commit "responsible" authorities to policies which provoke attacks on the status quo. The activities of United States capital interests in South America seem to have had this effect. The mere existence of monopolies with power to make arbitrary decisions on prices and the allocation of output, as for example in the case of the oil industry, is sufficient in itself to promote the perception of injustice even where injustice may not in fact exist.

## viii: Arms as a Cause of Conflict

Sir Edward Grey observed:

> The enormous growth of armaments in Europe, the sense of insecurity and fear caused by them—it was these that made war inevitable. This, it seems to me, is the truest reading of history, and the lesson that the present should be learning from the past in the interest of future peace, the warning to be handed on to those who come after us.[8]

---

[7] See Titmuss, R.: *The Irresponsible Society.* Fabian Tract 323. (London: The Fabian Society; 1960).
[8] Tate, M.: *The Disarmament Illusion. The Movement for a Limitation of Armaments to 1907.* (New York: The Macmillan Co.; 1942), p. 36.

One of the corollaries of the acceptance of war as an instrument of government is that peace may best be secured by preparedness for war. To be effective in defense, national armaments must be adequate competitively. The competitive element and the danger of war through preparation for it were observed by Montesquieu, who referred to the contagious nature of competitive arming as "the new distemper" and foresaw that armies to preserve peace could in fact provoke war. Kant, in *Perpetual Peace*, provided that "standing armies shall be abolished in course of time," and by way of explanation: "for they are always threatening the states with war by appearing to be in constant readiness to fight. They incite the various states to out-rival one another in the number of their soldiers, and to this number no limit can be set." The dilemma was becoming obvious in the twentieth century when peace through strength led on two occasions to an arms race which did not prevent war, but on the contrary made a substantial contribution to its final outbreak in 1914 and 1939. In the first half of the twentieth century, as in all previous centuries, the dilemma could be resolved in favor of war. War was still the accepted final instrument of national policy, and a practical one. The degree to which arms as such caused conflict and war cannot be determined. Superimposed upon other causes of conflict, however, they no doubt made a significant contribution, at least in the final buildup of suspicion and of fear.

### 3. SUMMARY

Classification of causes of conflict shows their changing nature. There was commonly a revolt against the status quo by those who considered themselves prejudiced, and defensive reactions by those under threat, leading to armaments which further aggravated political conflict. While perception of injustice and of waning prestige tended once to relate to geographical discovery and to the rivalries of an expanding world in which nations sought to conquer and to hold, more recently power rivalries have had to be accommodated to the independent status of peoples formerly subjugated. The forms of conflict have altered. The struggle has been the winning of allegiance, rather than the conquering of territory. It is the internal organization of society which is constantly being challenged, both within the main rival powers and within the developing states whose allegiance they seek to win.

New devices have been introduced to meet the new circumstances, and economic and political substitutes have been found for military suppression. However, the nature of the conflict remains fundamentally the same. Furthermore, war has remained the recognized last resort for the defense of existing national interests, and for the preservation of international structures created by the dominant powers. The United Nations rests upon the national and international defense structures which were evolved, and were appropriate to, classical forms of power rivalry.

# 2

## The Problem Stated: Disarmament and International Organization

### 1. THE NUCLEAR STALEMATE

Once nuclear weapons were possessed by all the main industrial powers, the traditional procedures and structures designed to preserve the established order and to prevent war were inappropriate. For the first time in history, war against a great power was impractical as an instrument of national or international policy. As a consequence of nuclear weapons, the world order could not sensibly rest on structures which merely reduced the frequency of war. If civilization were to survive with any degree of certainty, war had to be eliminated. Nor could a world order rest on preparedness for war, because the dilemma inherent in this policy could no longer be resolved in favor of war

27

without the possibility of the total destruction of all parties concerned. Moreover, the accompanying devices traditionally employed for deterring war—balance of power and military alliances—had not even a theoretical application in a world situation in which several nations each had sufficient power to destroy all others.

Political scientists and politicians alike knew of no structures or means which could with certainty prevent conflict. The policies and processes of past centuries were challenged by nuclear weapons, but no alternatives were available. Increased attention was given, therefore, to the perfecting of the policy of peace through strength, and to the stabilizing of the dilemma situation. In the early fifties, serious strategic thinking and policy making emphasized the quest for a position of at least equality in striking power and in defense, and for the means of detecting surprise attack. Strategy called also for techniques by which wars in defense of local positions might be waged without danger of all-out war, for a more efficient exploitation of mutual fear, for a more efficient use of deterrents, and for other considerations which arose directly out of this central nuclear dilemma. Among those who made a contribution in this field were Kissinger (*Nuclear Weapons and Foreign Policy*), Hinterhoff (*Disengagement*), Roberts (*Russia and America*), Kennan (*Russia, the Atom and the West*), and other Americans working in the field of political science. Contributors to the *Bulletin of the Atomic Scientist* and physicists in general also concerned themselves with these pressing strategic-political studies. Less political and more scientific were the methodological approaches of Kaplan (*System and Process in International Politics*) and others who endeavored to systematize the study.

However, such efforts could make no contribution to the fundamental problems of peaceful relations; they sought merely to prevent open warfare. At best, the process of perfecting policies of peace through strength could delay, and in theory indefinitely, the coming of a crisis in which the dilemma of competitive arms might finally be resolved.

The process of the perfecting of policies could in practice also provoke a crisis, and make more likely its resolution finally in favor of war. Preventive measures, especially those involving air reconnaissance toward another nuclear power, and those seeking to retain strike and defense superiority in a constantly changing technical situation, are likely to increase and not to decrease the danger of war. A major technical "breakthrough" could trigger off a deliberate preventive war, and accidental war is a constant danger associated with most preventive measures. Improved techniques in strike and in defense, furthermore, contribute to an arms race to which there is no technical end, and which, at any rate in the prenuclear age, tends to increase the dangers of war. Political and physical scientists were endeavoring to deal with the immediate threat to world society. In doing so they were providing time for a more fundamental solution to the problems of conflict. But they were also incidentally heightening the dangers of accidental war.

Out of this dilemma, inherent in the policy of peace through strength, arose another, this one unique to the nuclear age. War had been previously employed (as a last resort and after failure of negotiation) in defense of vital national interests. In the nuclear age war was likely to be self-destructive; and there was, therefore, an emergent or secondary dilemma: self-destruction, on the one hand, or piecemeal loss of vital interests on the other. Many Western publicists and observers in the fifties expressed themselves in favor of resolving this dilemma, if necessary, in favor of war. The risk of death, it was held, was preferred to certain "slavery."

Aware of these problems scientists and politicians of all countries urged disengagement, weapons-test bans, and disarmament. Such a policy seemed the only escape. The common fear, the realization that every additional defensive measure increased the danger of nuclear war, was a powerful incentive for the making of agreements to abolish at least those weapons of war which could destroy civilized society everywhere. The Unilateralists of Great Britain, the studies and negotiations on weapon-test bans and disarmament, the peace movements of the fifties and sixties, were all a response to this situation.

## 2. DISARMAMENT

The call for disarmament has been made in past ages in the interests of economy, as a means of avoiding war, and on the basis of pure reason. In the nuclear age it is a call with an urgency; it is a plea for survival. As such it is well founded. The abolition of nuclear weapons would remove the risk of accidental warfare. The removal of the immediate danger of war could possibly provide a climate of opinion in which the negotiation of more fundamental disputes could take place. Agreements on fundamental issues and agreements to establish stable conditions of peace are probably impossible in the short term, while the danger to civilization is immediate; and, in the absence of disarmament, the spread of nuclear weapons to smaller countries would increase the danger of accidental or irresponsible nuclear war.

The basis of Soviet foreign policy in the fifties and into the sixties was the advocacy of complete and general disarmament, including all armed forces down to local police forces and even to the eventual abolition of military staffs. The West, led by the United States, accepted this objective. Any disagreement was on procedures. Even so, however, there was by 1960 an increasing appreciation on the Soviet side of the Western insistence upon inspection starting from a mutually agreed-upon date; and on the Western side there was a growing acceptance of the Soviet view that complete disarmament within a given time was technically more practical than stage-by-stage disarmament procedures.[1] There was by 1961 a basis of agreement, at least with regard to all matters which had been discussed and on which there had been disagreement. It was the declared policy of the Soviet and the United States in 1961 to press on with disarmament negotiations.

Yet, the history of disarmament would suggest that it was an international exercise in negotiation with no practical significance. Tate's study of negotiation to 1907[2] gives no reason to believe that nation states would agree upon arms abolition any more than upon boundary abolition. History since 1907 gives no reason to change this view. Indeed, in the nuclear era there are increased technical difficulties in disarmament. For instance, even

[1] The evidence of this was in the agreement reached at a "Pugwash" conference of scientists held in Moscow in December, 1960.
[2] Tate, M.: *The Disarmament Illusion* (New York: The Macmillan Co.; 1942).

31

though there were complete agreement on the objective of accomplishing disarmament within a stated period, and also on controls, there would nevertheless remain the probably insoluble technical problem of hidden-weapon detection; and this could make agreement impossible. Genuine technical difficulties, small and large, crop up at every stage of negotiation.

There are, furthermore, political difficulties which involve not merely the powers chiefly concerned. The Soviet demand for general and complete disarmament made at the General Assembly in 1960 was based on the claim that a world without arms is a world without war. This is true, however, only in a limited sense, for there are effective nonmilitary means of warfare for which all the main powers have the financial and diplomatic potential and skill. It is probable that even in a disarmed world this nonmilitary warfare would be waged, threatening spheres of influence and leading to rearmament. It is difficult to see how a leading power, no matter how impressed with the urgency of disarmament, could enter into a disarmament treaty without clear agreements and controls relating to a disarmed world. Smaller and middle powers would be hard to persuade that their territorial integrity was safeguarded merely by some form of international organization. Underdeveloped countries, over which Great-Power conflict is currently being waged, would provide a constant threat to peaceful relations. Agreements on nonmilitary means of warfare and the establishment of basic conditions of peace would seem to be matters for simultaneous negotiation, if not preconditions of negotiation.

Military disengagement, as distinct from disarmament, was another means suggested for solving the nuclear problem. Disengagement was intended merely to reduce the possibilities of conflict and the costs of armaments. However, disengagement proposals run counter to the whole waiting nature of the conflict, so well exposed by Rabinowitch:

> The political leaders of most nations understand that the arms race cannot last indefinitely, and that, sooner or later, a form of international existence must be found which would permanently exclude war. . . . However, they postpone acting for such a new world system until after the victory of their economic and political ideology, which they confidently expect to win.

Each side believes there are historic forces which will destroy the economy and political institutions of the other. "Neither side is swayed by examples—some of them quite recent—which obviously contradict their generalizations. Both play for time, in the hope that the other side bears seeds of inner instability, and will sooner or later collapse." [3]

Disarmament and disengagement proposals are predicated upon the assumption of an international force which would ensure international law and order. Consequently, the problems of international organization have first to be faced, for international organization is an integral part of disarmament plans. Without agreement on an international enforcement organization, disarmament plans are not likely to succeed; and agreement on such an organization remains unlikely.

The concept of world imperialism, or of universal organization in which states abrogate powers and allow

[3] *Bulletin of the Atomic Scientists*, Vol. XV, no. 1 (Jan., 1959), p. 4.

enforcement against them, is unreal. In the nuclear age it is not necessary for any industrially developed state to accept enforcement. It is indeed an international system of nations with full sovereign powers which has to be organized; and in such a system each state will retain its armed forces and defend its own interests unilaterally if necessary. This is a conclusion arrived at, after long analysis based on the theory of games, by Strausz-Hupé and Possony.[4]

> It may be concluded that international organizations, by their very nature as free associations of peoples and their inability to operate as authoritarian supergovernments, cannot effectively perform as war-preventing agencies. They are peace organizations in the double sense that they can function only in peacetime and that they should improve the cooperation between states. But if war were to threaten again, they would not be able to maintain peace. The only task which international organizations are equipped to fulfil is to strengthen the peace that exists.

In any event, even assuming that disarmament or disengagement were technically and politically possible, it would seem an act of madness for any leader to advocate disarmament while he still assumed (a) that the other side intended to aggress, as soon as the opportunity occurred, either directly into his country's territory or into areas of strategic importance in other parts of the world; (b) that the other side intended to destroy his country's system; and (c) that the other side would not carry out

[4] *International Relations* (New York: McGraw-Hill Book Co.; 1950), p. 850.

any agreements and would use any military or nonmilitary means available to it to achieve its aggressive purposes.

Neither the Communist nor the Western authorities and scientists who studied the problems involved made any attempt to face up to these incompatibilities in disarmament thinking. In the literature of the period there was little, if any, discussion of a disarmed world, despite a great deal of discussion on disarmament. No examination seems to have been made of how to resolve conflict in a disarmed world, of how spheres of influence would be controlled without leading to further political conflict, of how smaller and independent nations would be protected, or of other obvious and related problems of disarmament.

Presumably, the original sources of the communist-capitalist conflict were considered by both sides to be relatively unimportant compared with the constant threat of nuclear warfare. Certainly this belief must have been behind the British movements of the fifties for unilateral disarmament. For the United States to wish to stop shouldering the burden of the "Cold War" and to stop protecting smaller countries at the risk of a nuclear war would have been compatible with previous American isolationist and neutralist sentiments. There was, however, a second reason for considering disarmament without consideration of the post-disarmament world. The Communist countries considered that their objectives could be achieved without war, and by means of propaganda and organization. The West also, faced with the continued threat of nuclear war, and being by the late fifties far more confident in its own ability to compete in a neutralist Asia and Africa, seems to have been far readier to

35

accept the Communist challenge of nonmilitary competition than it had been in the forties when its policy was to meet political change anywhere by a threat of force.

At a discussion of scientists at the Pugwash Conference in 1960, Americans seemed to take the view that the United States was not equipped in terms of political institutions to continue to shoulder the burden of protecting the rest of the Western world, and of thus inviting every day the risk of destruction through war either by accident or by design. In their view, a disarmed world would lead to all kinds of political changes in the short term; but after a settling process a new balance would be struck. The Soviet scientists seemed to regard all thought of a postdisarmament world as irrelevant. In their view, disarmament was the only course which would avoid the nuclear threat, and consequential problems had to be faced as they arose. Neither side seemed to be concerned with the origins of their conflict, or with the problems of resolving conflict in a disarmed world.

However, many political scientists in the fifties were nevertheless questioning the wisdom of the disarmament approach which had been adopted on a political level. Eugene Rabinowitch questioned

the almost universal belief that disarmament is the most promising path to the creation of a stable and peaceful world. It seems to me that the hope that trust between nations can be increased by successive disarmament steps is very precarious. . . . This means, in the first place—creating the sense of common purpose. It can be argued that, in the meantime, further negotiations on disarmament may be

36

fraught with the danger of enhancing the existing distrust rather than reducing it.[5]

Tate has an historic perspective which is salutary:

> Armament competition is inextricably interwoven with political tension, and international agreement on armaments is possible only when the national policies of states are not in conflict; for international disarmament standardizes the relative diplomatic power of the countries involved and prevents the use of armaments competition to upset the political equilibrium. . . . Arms could not be limited without perpetuating a settlement intolerable to several states. . . . For the maintenance of the status quo involves the perpetuation of a settlement unjustly imposed by the power of the sword. . . .[6]

Lord Russell, with characteristic realist-idealism, comments:

> There are many who consider that the problem of agreed disarmament or reduction of armaments is the most important in the field of international relations and the one to be first dealt with. I do not share this view. Needless to say, I consider agreed reduction of armaments very important and I favour the complete prohibition of all nuclear weapons, whether strategic or tactical. I see, however, two objections to treating this as the central and primary problem: first, as the experience of the last thirteen years has shown, disarmament conferences cannot

[5] *Bulletin of the Atomic Scientist,* Vol. XVI, no. 2 (Feb., 1960), p. 37.
[6] Tate, M.: op. cit., pp. 346, 347.

reach agreements until the relations of East and West become less strained than they have been; second, the long-run problem of saving mankind from nuclear extinction will only be postponed, not solved, by agreements to renounce nuclear weapons. Such agreements will not, of themselves, prevent war, and, if a serious war should break out, neither side would consider itself bound by former agreements, and each side would, in all likelihood, set to work to manufacture new H-bombs as quickly as possible.[7]

Kennan agrees with this view:

> It is true that armaments can and do constitute a source of tension in themselves. But they are not self-engendering. No one maintains them just for the love of it. They are conditioned at bottom by political differences and rivalries. To attempt to remove the armaments before removing these substantive conflicts of interests is to put the cart before the horse . . .[8]

Apart from the practical and political difficulties of a negotiated disarmament, disarmament does not provide a solution to problems of conflict. Disengagement, weapons-test bans, and disarmament are emergency measures to be taken because of the emergency situation. No more can be claimed for them; they do not solve the basic problem. An immediate danger may be for a time avoided, but there is no guarantee that rearmament will not take

[7] Russell, B.: *Common Sense and Nuclear Warfare* (London: Geo. Allen & Unwin, Ltd.; 1959), p. 46.
[8] Kennan, G.: *Russia, the Atom and the West* (Oxford: Oxford University Press; 1958), p. 29.

place. The basic problems which were the cause of the armaments remain, even though arms, themselves one cause of war, are removed. Furthermore, a disarmed world provides no final defense of interests against nonmilitary aggression. In the absence of any means of peaceful adjustment, piecemeal loss of vital interests remains a problem, leading to rearmament and to the return of the emergent nuclear dilemma.

The result was that by 1961 there appeared a completely confused set of incompatible policy motivations. In his first State-of-the-Nation Message to Congress in January 1961, President Kennedy reminded the nation that the original aims of communism for world domination still held. He announced a program of increased defense and retaliation power (perhaps not unconnected with the unemployment then current in the steel industry). At the same time he assured the nation that he would co-operate with the Communists as far as possible to reduce tension, and he would press forward with disarmament negotiations. On the Communist side, peaceful relations were stated to be the main aim and disarmament a necessity; but claims were still made that by one means or another socialist states had to be created universally before there could be peace.

There was thus a complete impasse. A nuclear war, premeditated, accidental, or irresponsible, remained a possibility. Even assuming that civilized society were to survive a nuclear war, there are still no known and agreed foundations on which a peaceful world society could be built. Indeed, given the assumptions made by early philosophers regarding the origins of the state and the need for state arms, given technical developments throughout the ages up to the discovery of nuclear energy, the nuclear

39

impasse is the logical and inevitable outcome of any society organized on a state basis. On these assumptions
a fresh start, even with foreknowledge of the final outcome, would produce the same results.

The appeals of the lawyers for the outlawing of war
seem more politically relevant; but as Julius Stone, a law-
yer himself, demonstrated, solutions along these lines beg
the main questions. "It is demands for abolition of weapons and for inauguration of 'the rule of law' (not to
speak of the establishment of a World State) which promote and cater to sentimentalism, loose-mindedness and
chimeric dreaming." [9]

In circumstances such as these, a revision of fundamental thinking on the problem of war is provoked; no
further refinements of the balance of power or of the mu-
tual-terror theory can contribute more than a temporary
respite. In this sense the nuclear weapon has brought
about a change in the nature of the problem of war; it
has forced a complete rethinking of all assumptions, theories, and preconceived notions.

The problem remains one of organizing international
relations in ways which enable independent nations to
obtain their maximum competitive satisfactions. The
competition is inevitable. Its effective control has yet to
be devised. The conflict between communism and capitalism cannot be resolved without finding ways in which
further adjustments can be made by peaceful means. The
problem is to determine the nature of a disarmed world,
for without this there cannot be disarmament. This
means determining a condition of peace.

A field of noxious weeds, weeds of the species *arma-*

[9] "Law and Policy in the Quest for Survival," *The Australian Broadcasting Commission Lectures* (1960).

*ment,* can be cleared by cutting them out with a hoe. It is a direct and satisfying method and seems to be a sensible one. It is possible to plan area by area and to agree, with neighbors who fear the spread of such seed, to complete one's own field for their inspection over a certain period if they will do the same. Next year it will be necessary to do the same again, and the next and the next, for under this system the seed is still in the ground. A far more scientific method, on the other hand, leads with scientific certainty to quicker achievement, though it may appear to be less direct. The weeds are hoed out—though this is not necessary except to show good faith to neighbors in the first year. In the meantime the soil is examined to see why weeds dominated in the first place; and those trace elements or preconditions of *useful* growth are ascertained which are missing. The soil is then built up as required; and the seed of useful crops is introduced, of the species *co-operation in underdevelopment,* or something similar. The weeds not only find the reconditioned soil unhealthy, but they cannot compete with the new crop. In practice the only difficulty with this scientific procedure is that the farmer is a conservative person, accustomed to hoeing and to suffering crop losses through weed growth, and slow to understand that his old method cannot succeed.

### 3. THE BREAKDOWN OF INTERNATIONAL ORGANIZATION

Traditionally, international organization has had the responsibility of ensuring the observation of accepted principles, and if necessary the enforcement of its decisions upon members whose actions appeared to be threatening world peace or world structure. Traditionally, international organization has been created in the image of the administration of a federal system of states.

As such it has been centralized. The United Nations, after the model of the League of Nations, was created as a centralized body, at least in its political activities. The whole burden of decision making and of enforcement was carried in particular by the Security Council and the Secretary-General. Every dispute, no matter how trivial or how local, came before the central organization. By the time it was referred to the Security Council it was at an advanced stage, frequently one of open conflict.

This burden was too great for a centralized United Nations to carry. It was, primarily, an administrative burden. The proceedings of the United Nations, and in particular those of the Security Council, could originally be followed in detail by responsible national leaders; adequate responsible attention and direction could be given. In the course of ten years, however, it became an organization which met almost continuously, dealing with many minor disputes arising out of local circumstances not understood by most nations. It was impossible for national leaders to follow proceedings, and delegates frequently acted without responsible instruction. This in turn encouraged bloc voting, the uncritical acceptance of the leadership of a friendly Great Power which, it was assumed, knew the facts. In these circumstances it was not surprising that the United Nations became a forum at which nationalistic and improvised points of view were expressed in propaganda terms.

The central staff of the United Nations became immersed in the details of world affairs and tied to a routine which effectively prevented the imaginative leadership and advice which should be expected of an international secretariat. The routine of the United Nations, the day-by-day work and responsibilities, placed a burden on the Secretary-General probably greater than that carried by the political head of any government. He had no responsible cabinet with whom to share the burden.

Furthermore, the advantages of decentralization, now widely appreciated in the field of domestic administration, were wholly lacking. In the Congo instance of 1960-1, to give only one of many examples, the Secretary-General and his staff were required at a moment's notice to make recommendations to and carry out the decisions of the Security Council on matters about which they could not be informed fully and which more appropriately would have been dealt with, in the first instance at least, by a regional body acquainted with local circumstances. In dealing with the complex subject matter of international political relations, it is impossible for a central organization to be fully advised and to act with the necessary wisdom.

The original intention of the United Nations Charter was to promote forms of regionalism by which there would be local association between governments in the same area, as a means of preventing conflict and of resolving it when it occurred. This was the purpose of Chapter VIII of the Charter, which dealt with Regional Arrangement. (See Chapter 4, Note 2, for the full text.) However, for reasons to be given, no regional arrangements designed to settle disputes were developed. The consequence of the existence, on the one hand, of military alliances, and of the absence, on the other, of arrangements concerned with eliminating conflict, was that the whole burden of peaceful settlement of disputes, together with the consequences of competitive arming arising out of military alliances, placed upon the central international organization a burden for which it was not designed.

These two administrative difficulties, the enormous quantity of business which prevented responsible national supervision, and the complexity of the subject matter on which the Secretariat could not adequately be informed, were both increased by additional membership. The inclusion by 1960 of fifty new members in addition to the original fifty rendered the body ineffective as a deliberative, fact-finding, conflict-resolving organization. In addition to the administrative problems, and arising out of this centralized administrative structure, there were grave political difficulties. Local disputes in their origin frequently do not concern other powers. They would more easily be resolved by local argument, or local argument could define the issues for decision by the Security Council. But in the centralized organization, local disputes became extended and confused. They reflected and aggravated already existing rivalries among the Great Powers.

The centralized international organization of the United Nations, operating in the absence of constructive regional bodies and in a world environment dominated by military alliances, itself contributed thus to the aggravation of conflicts and to their spread. Its operations threatened even its own existence by 1960. The world organization as a structure was being challenged as irrelevant to the times; and alterations, probably impracticable in themselves but revealing dissatisfaction with the organization, were being suggested.

### 4. THE FUNDAMENTAL PROBLEM

It would be fallacious to argue that merely because human survival demands a solution to the problem of resolving conflict, a solution must exist. It would be no less fallacious to argue, on the other hand, that no solution exists merely because the experience of past ages indicates the virtual inevitability of conflict, and of war as the final means of resolving conflict.

Most political scientists in the nuclear era have concentrated, with a sense of urgency, on deterrence and other means of avoiding nuclear war, without paying special attention to the more difficult problem of resolving conflict. Their studies have not led to any satisfying conclusions. Rethinking is now required of the general problem of conflict. No less fundamental an approach is likely to make a significant contribution to the problem of avoiding nuclear war. The problem of war is not fundamentally changed by the introduction of new weapons; whether bows and arrows, cannon, high explosives, or nuclear weapons, the problem relates back to social behavior and to social organization. War, conventional or nuclear, either can or cannot be avoided. Early philosophers seemed to think it could not, at least in their day. In the nuclear era we are forced to re-examine the whole problem in the circumstances of our day, with no preconceived notions which could constitute an inheritance from a world of wholly different political or social circumstances.

A similar problem has been faced before. The unemployment of the thirties was no different in character from the unemployment which had previously been experienced for centuries in Europe. In the Middle Ages it had been possible to maintain political and economic stability by whipping and gaoling "sturdy beggars," a policy deriving logically from the theory that unemployment was due to laziness. In the seventeenth century the Poor Laws treated unemployment as a social rather than an individual problem. Nevertheless, the main concern was still to maintain an official financial stability by cutting budgets in times of recession, a policy following logically from the belief that political economy was no different in kind from domestic housekeeping. If in practice further unemployment developed, the scale was still such that it could be dealt with by direct unemployment legislation and repressive measures. However, the scale of unemployment in the thirties forced a search for the theoretical fallacies; it could not be dealt with by traditional financial or legislative methods. A situation existed which could not be allowed to occur again, for it would be politically fatal to whatever government was in power. There was a basic query: was there error in past thinking, or was unemployment inevitable? Upon re-examination, appropriate financial remedies were found which were the reverse of past policies; an expansion of expenditure and of budgets, not a contraction, was found to be the means of re-employing idle men. The significance of the Great Depression was that it provided the stimulus and the opportunity for a complete rethinking of theory and of policy, in a political atmosphere in which there was a far greater acceptance of analytical and radical thinking. The problem of unemployment itself had not changed. Its extent had revealed fallacies in past thinking, and paved the way for a new approach. The remedies suggested were not relevant exclusively to the Great Depression, but were equally applicable to earlier periods of unemployment and to any future recessions.

46

And so it is with the problem of war in the nuclear age.


In these two introductory chapters, an attempt has been made to state the problem. Power rivalry has remained fundamentally the same, despite most important changes in its nature and in the techniques employed. But the invention of weapons of mass destruction, and their possession by all main powers, has made wholly inappropriate the national policies and international structures which have been evolved over the ages to defend an existing order and to change it when an alteration is demanded. Nevertheless, we still adhere to these outmoded policies and structures. Attempts have been made to make them more efficient so that they will prevent nuclear warfare; but these attempts are likely to be self-defeating. A complete rethinking of international relations is required. War, once accepted as inevitable or as a necessary evil, has to be eliminated. Traditional concepts and thought processes have to be challenged. The search is no longer for machinery for reducing the possibilities and incidence of war, but for means of eliminating conflict within an international system which is fundamentally competitive. Hence we now turn to examine the basic nature of conflict, and to try to discover what constitutes a condition of peace among competitive sovereign states.

# 3

## The Dynamics of Conflict

### 1. A CONDITION OF PEACE AS A FUNCTION OF CHANGE

A condition of peaceful international relations is not a condition of equilibrium; no static concept is relevant to relations between and among nations. The study of peaceful international relations is not the study of a peaceful relationship destroyed by change and later re-established after adjustments have taken place, along the lines of the equilibrium analysis of economics. It is the study of a relationship in which change continuously takes place, but by means which do not necessarily destroy a condition of peace. The condition of peace is, therefore, itself a function of change and of adjustment to it. Consequently, the starting point of peace theory is an examination of change and of responses to change, rather than an examination of a hypothetical and static position of peaceful relations.

## 2. THE REVOLUTIONARY AND THE STATUS QUO

With almost every change, clashes of interest are likely to occur, for most change favors one nation relatively more than others, or causes more hardship to one nation than to others. Discovery favored Portugal, Spain, and Britain; industrialization in Japan prejudiced the interests of the British textile trade; the philosophy of Marx assisted Russia; the independence movement weakened British overseas interests; and synthetics reduced the market for producers of natural products.

For the sake of exposition in tracing the effects of change,[1] R (revolutionary) is used to designate the coun-

[1] In describing the relationships among nations, their responses to change, and reactions to these responses, most complicated patterns of behavior have to be considered. In this exposition these relationships have been simplified by referring to S and R countries as though there were only one change taking place at a time, and as though only two countries were affected. In practice many important changes take place at once. All countries are static in relation to some and dynamic in relation to others. All are reacting both passively and actively. All absorb and resist change to some degree. The language of everyday use, even in the hands of the most gifted, is inadequate for an accurate description of such a complex pattern. As peace theory develops, precision will demand the invention of terms and phrases relevant to it.

S has been used to represent a state interested in preserving existing conditions against change, and R the state in which change was taking place. $S + R$ could represent the unstable relationship which exists between the two, a potential state of conflict. If S responds to change in a retaliatory way, this could be represented by $S^a$, with degrees of retaliation to $S^n$, and R reactions could be similarly described. The cumulative reactions of each lead ultimately to an open conflict situation, $S^n + R^n$. If S defended itself against the effects of change, but by means which did not provoke aggressive responses in R, then this would be represented by $S^{pa} \rightarrow {}^{pn}$, leading to a peaceful relationship, $S^{pa} \rightarrow {}^{pn} = R$. If S were to absorb completely the effects of change, this could be represented by xS, leading to a peaceful relationship, $xS = R$. In practice the S response is likely to be some absorption, some passive defense, and some aggressive

try in which the change occurs, and S (status quo) the country which is affected adversely by the change and which may wish for this reason to resist or to prevent it. In using these concepts, we must keep in mind that some changes in R, for example a drought, might benefit S and be prejudicial to the interests of R. It does not follow that R is always the beneficiary of change, or that S is always adversely affected. However, as change is in many cases an invention or a deliberate national development, it can be assumed that most often it will benefit the nation in which it occurs. For convenience in exposition we are assuming that this is the case.

In some cases negotiation between R and S enables a passive response by S that is a complete absorption of, and adjustment to, the effects of the change. This was

---

response. In the absence of any aggressive response, a condition of peace is thus $xS^{pa} \to {}^{pn} = yR^{pa} \to {}^{pn}$. We noted that it was possible for conflict situations to arise out of the existence of arms and of traditional views of aggressive ideologies, even though adjustments had been made, and the original conflict had virtually been resolved. Then this condition of peace as described could be superimposed on an $S^n + R^n$ situation.

For convenience, then, S refers to those nations which together are on the defensive against change, and R to those nations which are the initiators of change. A major conflict usually resolves itself, in due course, in political warfare between two power blocs, and the symbols could be regarded as representing all the nations within each bloc. But there is no such alignment at an early stage of conflict, and each nation responds differently to the same change. Furthermore, each nation is both R and S in relation to changes taking place simultaneously. Each absorbs some change, responds passively to some, and resists some. Translated into national terms, when each of 100 nations is in a peaceful relationship with every other nation, a condition of peace is $xN(R/S)^{pa} \to {}^{pn} = yN^2 \to {}^{100} (S/R)^{pa} \to {}^{pn}$.

The task of the political scientist is to describe pa → pn responses, to determine the characteristics of x absorption, and to ascertain the conditions which are necessary in the international environment to ensure that these passive responses are those which in fact take place.

the case, for example, when the United States sold cheaply or gave surplus wheat to needy Asian countries after some good seasons in the fifties, and appeared to threaten the markets of normal exporters to that area. Conflict was resolved, and a stable S/R relationship resulted.

It will be noted that the term "adjustment" is being used as meaning accommodation, an adaptation to new circumstances, an acceptance of change. It is given a positive connotation. This is its proper meaning: "to harmonize, to settle, to be adjusted" [O.E.D.]. Not all responses and reactions are an adjustment. The term is here used in contradistinction to responses which are a reaction *against* change, an attempt to prevent its taking place, a retaliation against those originating it, or a refusal to make adjustments.

Generally speaking, the response by other countries to extensive economic and political change is rarely passive, and internal adjustment does not take place. Men and materials are not easily transferred from one industry to another, trade terms are not quickly adjusted, political thinking does not respond readily to new ideas, conflicts of interests are not resolved by any automatic devices or by any effective institutions of conciliation and arbitration. Changes most usually have some side effects and some political repercussions, leading to defensive and retaliatory policies directed against the cause of the change.

If for any reason the response of S is to resist or to prevent the change, there will be some frustration experienced by R. This is the case, for instance, when R initiates some moves toward independence or a change in government, and S, believing it not to be in its interests, acts to prevent this. Or, taking another example, S might react against a technical change in R by employing discriminatory tariffs (that is, tariffs directed specifically against R, not nondiscriminatory and applying to all countries). S may react to changes in political thinking by erecting barriers to cultural and political contact with R, or by threatening countermeasures and regional alliances. Then R, the nation in which the change originally took place and which therefore provoked the reaction by S, becomes the aggrieved and frustrated party. Its maximum opportunities for development, increased by the change, have been frustrated by a nation which chose protection and countermeasures rather than internal adjustment to and absorption of the change. Latent conflict has thus developed.

S, which is inconvenienced by change in the first place and which could with some emotion, therefore, if not reason, regard itself as having a grievance, is a cause of political tension through its failure to make necessary adjustments. Its defensive actions have imposed restraints on the nation initiating the change. It has provoked by its own reactions further retaliatory change by R. The form of the R reaction may be political protest, retaliatory discrimination, or some such gesture of frustration.

It can be seen, therefore, that in the real world it is not change as such which creates conflict, but the failure of S to accept change and to make adjustment to it in ways which permit the fulfillment of increased potentialities by R. It follows that any device introduced into international relations which tends to prevent change, or more especially to make unnecessary adjustment to change—for example, a balance of power, an international force, a superior national force, or the threat of a deterrent—creates a situation of frustration and of nonpassive response. While there may not be any immediate political or military reactions, depending upon the effectiveness of the device, in due course an accumulation of nonadjustment and of frustrated national objectives is likely to provoke political or military reaction from even the weakest of nations. In the presence of any such device the relationship between S and R is inherently unstable. In the real world there are many changes and responses to change occurring simultaneously and continuously, and affecting directly many different countries in different ways. A complicated relationship among S and R countries reflecting varying degrees of conflict would be a normal condition of international relations. In fact, the real position is even more complicated. Each nation is in some respects static in relation to some changes, and revolutionary in relation to other concurrent changes. Furthermore, there will be at least some degree of absorption of change by each nation. Major conflicts tend, however, to resolve into groupings of nations, and open conflict tends finally to emerge in a relatively simple relationship between two power blocs. The oversimplified concept of an S/R relationship is, therefore, satisfactory for purposes of exposition at this stage.

### 3. PRIMARY CHANGE

Whether the S response is passive or not ought reasonably to depend upon the extent of the effects on S of the change in question; but in actual practice the S response can be more materially influenced by any one of a number of local and temporary circumstances. For instance, the response can depend upon the amount of previous experience in negotiation which has taken place between R and S, the existence or absence of other common interests, the organizational level of vested interests in the S countries, and the assistance given by governments to industry to effect or to resist change. The response can depend upon the buoyancy of economic conditions, the stage of cultural and political development, and the kinds of administrative and political institutions. It can depend upon the support which S countries might expect from other unaffected but friendly countries, in the event that adjustments are resisted and political conflict becomes serious.

The nature of the change, especially its motivation, and the perception of the motivation are important. For this reason it is useful to distinguish between primary and secondary change. By primary change is meant geographical, geological, biological, and other changes in the natural environment brought about with or without man's deliberate activity. Besides these natural changes, the term "primary change" is used to include changes consequent upon discovery, invention, innovation, population increases deliberately sponsored, new social teachings, rates of development in cultural and economic levels, and all other types of change which are normal domestic processes. The characteristic of primary change is that its effect on other nations is transmitted only incidentally in the usual course of international relations; the attribute which is of significance about it is not its naturalness, but rather its domestic significance and nature. For instance, industrialization in one country changes international relationships, but this is not the intent. The discovery of a new process might prejudice the interests of producers elsewhere, but this would be quite accidental.

### 4. SECONDARY CHANGE

Acts by governments which are, on the other hand, deliberately intended to alter economic, social, political, strategic, or other interstate relationships, we shall term "secondary." Deliberate acts to *prevent* alterations are also, in a dynamic world, reasonably included in this category of secondary change. The term "secondary" is selected because such deliberate acts of governments are frequently responses to natural and other primary change. For instance, when invention (primary change) leads to cheaper production costs in R, and S resists adjustments and endeavors to prevent the effects of change, secondary change has been initiated. R is likely to retaliate (further secondary change) if opportunity occurs, and in the meantime to regard itself as being prejudiced by S responses.

These categories are not mutually exclusive. A stimulated population growth, which could be described as "primary," could be designed to alter strategic relationships, and repression of a domestic political party is likely to be a policy directed against some foreign country. The two categories are, however, in practice distinguishable, as will be seen in the course of the analysis.

International reactions do not arise out of the nature of change. It is the *perception by other nations* of the nature of change which determines their responses. The same change may be perceived differently by different nations, and differently by the same nation at different times, and there may be a variety of responses. Generally, however, change designed to injure another party is perceived by that party as such, and change which injures merely incidentally is perceived as such. Although it is perception that is the stimulus to response, and not the

55

change, there are nevertheless categories of change likely to be perceived as being deliberately injurious, and others not likely to be so perceived. While mindful of the role of perception, it is important from the point of view of policy to be able to differentiate between those actions which tend to provoke and those which generally do not provoke retaliatory responses. For this reason the concept of primary and secondary change can play a useful role in the development of peace theory, and an examination of these different types of changes will be found rewarding in an understanding of the dynamics of conflict.

5. CUMULATIVE CHANGE

Awareness of attempts by other nations to absorb change and to make some passive adjustments could delay reactions by R to countermeasures by S. If in the case of Japanese industrial growth there had been, at an early stage of conflict, some real evidence of attempts to accommodate cheap Japanese production, and not merely to prevent Japanese products from coming onto the international market, the military responses of Japan might not have developed.

Once conflict emerges, however, once there is failure to adjust passively to change, cumulative factors operate at an ever increasing rate, finally leading to an arms race and possibly to a situation approaching open warfare. The frustration reaction of the revolutionary and the anxiety reaction of the countries on the defensive are in themselves change which may promote further change. One of the most frequent types of policy which promote cumulative change is defensive action to offset the effects of change. Such action promotes further change of the same order. This was the case before the nature of depressions was understood, and when restrictive credit policies merely increased the need for further restrictive policies. In the political field there is a certain attractive logic about resisting a force by backing the opposite force. In the period after World War II attempts were made in Asia by the West to back the extremes of feudalism as a means of combatting communism. This merely provoked further resentment, and as a consequence there was need to give even stronger backing to feudalism, including military assistance.

In this way there accumulates a need for a vast amount of adjustment. The existence of iron curtains, barriers to contact which both sides erect over a period of years, creates a condition of mutual ignorance of the developments which take place in both S and R. Education, propaganda, official statements, restrictions on movement, all contribute to isolation and to protection against influence. Security measures, aimed primarily at preventing such influence and debarring any encroachments on the part of the institutions of the other bloc, are effective in delaying and preventing the normal compromises and adjustments which take place when any two societies are in contact. Such security measures prevent adjustments not only in the leading nations, but also, so far as is possible, in the smaller countries in their sphere of influence. Commerce and trade force some adjustments, but political contact is deliberately restricted. The adjustments required for negotiation, for mutual understanding of the other's position, for reliable anticipation of policy, and for an awareness of changes as they occur in each other's institutions, become so tremendous as to be politically impossible.

57

The political and academic literature of the fifties abounds with statements, made in good faith and made as though they were objective statements of fact, which are full of prejudice and subjective judgment based to a large degree on the propaganda of the day. Scientists no less than politicians took any conciliatory approach on the part of the other bloc as a trick, or as an attempt to play for time. Serious negotiation was impossible. C. Wright Mills was provoked to comment:

> . . . like quarrelling children, their reasoning is often reduced to mere assertion and counterassertion. The arguments of leading intellectual circles about war and peace often seem merely another turn in the cold-war rhetoric that now passes in East, in West, and in between, for public discourse. They are without orientation to considered values, and without guidance of clarifying definition.[2]

A group at Stanford University is seeking to ascertain the step-by-step process by which a conflict, once begun, eventually reaches the stage of open warfare. Basing their research on World War I, they are endeavoring to trace each statement of policy by R, the perception by S of each of these statements, and R's perception of statements by S. Different kinds of perception are being examined— accurate interpretation, hostile, friendly, and other kinds. It is an attempt to ascertain precisely the stages by which a statement of future policy by R is perceived by S as a threat, to which R responds by an imperative declaration of action to be taken in stated circumstances, which dec-

[2] Mills, C. Wright: *The Causes of World War Three* (London: Secker and Warburg; 1959), p. 14.

laration S perceives as virtually a declaration of war. S therefore takes the necessary precautionary steps, to which R responds by open warfare. This behaviorist approach may prove a most important contribution to the understanding of conflict. It shows, moreover, that mere declarations and their perception are sufficient, without any aggressive actions, to promote warfare.

### 6. SELF-GENERATING SECONDARY CHANGE FACTORS

Once the conflict has promoted an arms race, the original conflict situation is overshadowed by the immediate military threats, suspicions, misunderstandings, and other results of the cumulative process. The existence of effective striking power by either party is in itself, and without any other factor in the relationship between S and R, justification for the striking power of the other. Without any other changes, changes in striking power, or even a theoretical change in military technology, could lead to open warfare.

It follows that it is theoretically possible for conflict between S and R to reach a stage approximating open warfare, even though there have been in the meantime adjustments which removed the original basis of conflict. Open warfare could in practice be superimposed on a situation in which there had been complete adjustment to and absorption of change. The latter situation is likely to develop if during the building up of the conflict there have been negotiations, recognition of claims, changes in social philosophy, and generally a process of integration through conflict (the process by which negotiations and experience enables S and R to alter interpretations and perceptions of the actions and statements of each other).

This means that open warfare is possible for reasons which may have no relationship to the original dispute. Germany in 1939 had opportunities to win the type of economic and other agreements which, objectively (and in terms of German statements of German problems presented by German academicians to the Bergen Studies Conference of 1939) were necessary in order to remove the limitations imposed on its economic development by the previous peace treaties and by the consequences of the Great Depression. Offers of nondiscrimination were made to Japan, very late it is true, and after military planning was well advanced. But once R has set a course of nonpassive adjustment, once ideological considerations begin to play an effective part as motivation, it seems that it is impossible to accept compromises or to be satisfied with the achievement of the original objectives by non-military means. The objective requirements of R seem to be submerged in local political and military movements, and the revolt against the status quo seems to be an end in itself, rather than a means to the original purpose of the revolt.

It could be that in 1939 there had not been sufficient adjustments and recognition by the S powers of the problems faced by the R powers to justify the acceptance of negotiation. There was "appeasement" in relation to Germany, but this was not recognition of basic problems; it was merely the acceptance of military aggression. Japan's problems received recognition for the first time in discussions which Mr. Hull had with a Japanese envoy, but only after war had begun against Britain and allied countries, and a few hours before war began against the

United States.[3] Japan's problems were in fact recognized after the war, and what Japan had fought for originally was finally accorded to her as part of the postwar settlement. This development was made possible by the extensive postwar study given to problems of reconstruction by a series of conferences (Food and Agriculture, Monetary, I.L.O., the Charter Conference, and others) at which the interdependence of economies was recognized as being of political as well as of economic importance.

## 7. INTEGRATIVE CHANGE

Increasing tension is not inevitably a continuous process. Changing perceptions, passive responses which are made possible by some changed circumstance, and integration through conflict, can lead to reductions in tension. In the nuclear age, some stabilization of an advanced position of tension, or even some withdrawal from it, has resulted from the fear of nuclear war. An advanced position can be followed by a less advanced state of tension. Far more study of actual situations would be required to ascertain the factors which bring about this result—for instance, changes of governments, sympathy through national disaster, increased knowledge or improved publicity, and so on. The existence of such factors, however, means that there is no inevitable trend toward open warfare.

After World War I, conflict developed between Communist Russia and the Western capitalist powers. During the twenty-year period which followed, there were immense changes—economic, sociological, and philosophi-

[3] See White Paper. Tabled in the Australian House of Representatives. (Dec. 16, 1941).

cal—within both power groups; and it is possible that the original conflict was to a large degree modified. Nevertheless, the cumulative processes continued to an approximation of open conflict as though there had been no basis for resolving the original problems.

The resistance by Western powers to the original Communist power in Russia is a matter of history. Their motivation stemmed from a combination of many factors, but may have been primarily a balance-of-power reaction to a growing state. This resistance was, in the period after World War II, not fundamentally changed by the fact that Russia and the West had been allies in the war against Germany and Japan. The emergence of China as a second great Communist power, and the postwar independence movements of Asia and the Middle East, re-enforced Western prewar attitudes toward communism.

The revolutionary power was demanding free opportunity to pursue national interests, to develop industrially and politically as it wished, and to export its cultural patterns and ideology to all countries, at least in open competition with others who would also be promoting their own. (It is characteristic of a revolutionary, insecure and fearful of counterrevolution, to deny to the S power the rights of competition it demands for itself.) Demands for independence and self-determination in non-Communist areas and the rise of new political institutions provided the main changes of the period, and determined the type of resistance to change. There was a far greater concern in world politics with ideology than was the case between the two wars.

In different circumstances the S powers might well have gone to war even in the forties and fifties to prevent the upset of the status quo. If there had been an accurate estimation of future industrial progress, if the revolutionary had not such a degree of ideological support and of popular sympathy in various parts of the world, if Communist aggression had been the military aggression of Hitler, if there had been no nuclear weapons, and if military and strategic problems had been those of the last century, "preventive" war might have taken place. Indeed, official statements by the United States at the time of the Korean War, and before Soviet possession of thermonuclear weapons, indicated that this was contemplated at least by some Western policy makers.

However, the West did not go to war, even though in terms of nuclear superiority it was in a position to do so. The nuclear dilemma of the late fifties then confronted both sides with a military stalemate. The economic development of the revolutionary countries continued to take place. The frustrations which originally had caused conflict, the policies designed to restrain Russian developments and to discourage communism, no longer existed.

In the meantime, adjustment and integration through conflict continued. Ever since the East-West conflict first appeared, immediately after World War I, there had been an acceptance of change by the West, both in domestic policies and in relation to overseas communities. There had been, moreover, basic changes in Western political philosophies. The extent of these changes has even yet not been fully assessed in political science. Among the symptoms of basic change are the following: the acceptance of the principles of the Charter of the United Nations, and those actual decisions of the United Nations which acknowledge the rights of self-determination and of equality of treatment; the decisions of the United States Government in respect to the treatment of Negroes; the tremendous economic-aid programs of the fifties; refugee relief; social legislation in modern Western states after the thirties; nondiscriminatory educational systems; and all the other innovations of the twentieth century which reflected a human, and not merely a legal interpretation of justice. After World War II the West made remarkable adjustments in policies on independence and colonialism. British colonies obtained their independence, and there was a growing tolerance of new forms of government.

Changes taking place in the first half of the twentieth century, including rapid industrialization, invention, and sociological change, were on a scale which made change itself a factor of little less significance than the subsequent discovery of nuclear energy. It altered power relationships and challenged the adequacy and accuracy of past thinking in much the same way as did nuclear energy. The development in a period of a quarter of a century of Russia and China as Communist states with a practical potential as great as any other state, and the emergence of many new and independent states, were in themselves both evidence of, and at the same time a further stimulus to the acceptance of, changes in sociological thinking quite revolutionary in themselves.

These two outstanding developments of the twentieth century, nuclear weapons and sociological development, were not related in origin. Nevertheless, in the sense that nuclear weapons made obsolete the traditional techniques of maintaining the status quo, they may have contributed to sociological and political development. For instance, the failure in the fifties of collective security, through the South East Asia Treaty Organization, to prevent political change in the area previously known as Indo-China, and the failure of the British-French attempt in 1956 to protect their interests in the Suez Canal, may both have been due in part to the dangers of nuclear warfare. Such an interpretation, however, takes no account of the earlier granting of independence to India, Ceylon, and Burma, and the movements which finally led to independence in Indonesia and Africa. In the absence of the nuclear threat, change was taking place even though other means of enforcement were available. The changes which took place in Indo-China and in Suez owed as much to the state of world public opinion, and to the prevalence of concepts of justice, as to any threat of warfare in the background. Perhaps events at this period mark a definite point in history at which human rather than legal justice prevailed. Expression of world public opinion at an international forum, the spread of ideas of independence made possible by wartime conditions, the effects of increased learning and communication, demands for higher living standards and the knowledge that such standards were possible, all contributed to change on a scale and of a type which destroyed any possibility of the defense of the status quo by national forces, or even by power balances.

There were, however, adjustments still to be made. The McCarthy-Dulles period of the forties and fifties in the United States set back this development and made it appear that the West was unwilling to make, or incapable of making, further adjustments to a new world situation. This was only a phase, however, and could not alter the longer-term trends which had persisted since the thirties. Not having gone to war when there was a clear nuclear advantage, and having made adjustments domestically and internationally, the S powers could no longer be regarded as static. Whatever the delays, the absorption of change was taking place.

Russia saw these changes. Some were to be regarded as partly a response to Communist pressures, some a response to postwar developments in national independence, some a natural development in political and sociological thinking. But the net result in any case was seen to be the independence of peoples and the development of the welfare state. The breakup of capitalism had not occurred as expected. Democracies seemed to be united, with strong worker support, and were achieving welfare ends by their own means. Depressions appeared to have been avoided and would not bring chaos to capitalism. And the nuclear weapon made total war impracticable. Some rethinking and adjustment were required, therefore, on the part of the Communist Powers.

Communist countries, Russia in particular, made internal adjustments. The internal political changes which took place in Russia during the fifties were undoubtedly a direct consequence of events and developments within Russia itself;[4] but it would be unrealistic to suggest that they had no relationship to the conditions of competition between the Great Powers. Greater liberalization appeared, and a rethinking of policies and attitudes seems to have occurred after observation of changes which had taken place in the capitalist countries. Evidence of this was in the dispute between Russia and China culminating in a conference in December 1960 and in a declaration in which there was acceptance of the Russian view that open warfare with capitalist states was not inevitable.

[4] See Boffa, G.: *Inside the Khrushchev Era* (London: George Allen & Unwin, Ltd.; 1960).

On both sides there was a clear recognition that change and adjustment were possible, and there was some willingness to pursue this course. On the other hand, the traditional structures of regional defenses and alliances designed to prevent change and adjustment still remained. The compromise formula offered by the Soviet was "peaceful coexistence," that is, a situation halfway between complete stability and complete instability. How this situation was to be maintained was not made clear. If coexistence meant the existence side by side in a dynamic world of two power blocs, neither of which would make any fundamental adjustments, then this was merely a recognition of continued conflict held in abeyance only by the nuclear deterrent. If by coexistence was meant coadaptation, that is, two organizations living side by side, carrying on normal international relations, and in due course making constant adjustments as a consequence of political and economic contacts, then this was a recognition that the original conflict was being eliminated. For political reasons neither side could afford to admit that the latter was possible or even desirable.

### 8. CHANGE IN THE REAL WORLD

For purposes of exposition, examples have been used to stress different types of change. In each of these there has been a combination of different types of change, trends toward increasing tension, and accompanying trends toward integration. The position in the sixties in the communist-capitalist competition was an advanced stage of tension. The original causes of conflict had been largely removed, or at least modified significantly. Russia was virtually uninhibited and unrestrained by S powers, unlike during the original period of conflict, and was making rapid progress economically and in international politics. Nevertheless, past Western policies, past attempts at restraint, and past declarations of intention were still relevant factors. There was still a sufficient vestige of past policies to aggravate the position and to reinforce the ingrained suspicion that the West still intended to act on the defensive as an S power. There were restraints on trade with Communist countries; there was still hostility toward China; there was persistent propaganda which condemned communism as a society. In the absence of a clear acceptance by the West of communism as a permanent society, and of a clear acknowledgment of its contributions to welfare, human responses ensured that the revolutionary would continue to react as if still frustrated by an identifiable agent and enemy. On the other side, to the West the Communist interpretation of coexistence seemed to spell piecemeal political aggression by means which the British and American political systems could not easily employ.

The political question for the R power is always this: to what extent must frustrations be worked out and overcompensated for, to what extent does revolution have to be carried before there is no further risk that S motivations will come again into action? Some Western decisions with respect to Korea, Indo-China, and other areas appeared to indicate that counterrevolution was still possible, as did also the establishment of SEATO and NATO. The political question for the S powers, in turn, is always as British Prime Minister Chamberlain found it in 1937 and 1938: to what extent can frustrations, once experienced, be allowed free expression and overcompensation without there being a vital threat to the interests of the S powers? In terms of human behavior, both sides tend to act with caution and anxiety. The critical point is passed in an ideological conflict when the revolutionary is willing to expose its system to the ideas of the status quo, and to permit the kind of adjustments and compromises which might follow, without experiencing the fear of counterrevolution; and when, on the other hand, the status-quo powers are so confident of meeting the challenge of the revolutionary without destruction of fundamental assets that they too are willing to remove protections and to allow free adjustment and compromise. This point may never be reached. Caution and over-caution on both sides lead to overcompensation by R and to the perception of aggression by S, resulting in progress toward a situation of open conflict even though the integrative process of coadaptation has been accomplished to an advanced stage.

# 4

# The
# Self-defeating Nature
# of Enforcement

## 1. A BEHAVIORIST STUDY

The relationship between S and R is essentially a behaviorist one. Whether there will be a cumulative development to an advanced position of tension out of some relatively simple change affecting relationships depends upon the nature of responses—passive and absorbing on the one hand, or active and retaliatory on the other. This in turn depends not merely on the extent of change, the real problems of adjustment involved, and the damage to interests which might result, but also on a great many psychological responses to the situation. For instance, response is likely to depend on whether the cause of change took place in a friendly or unfriendly country, whether

70

the change appeared to be a deliberate attempt to prejudice the interests of other nations or merely an accident, whether it took place in a period of tension caused by other events, and many other such circumstances.

The characteristic feature of the S and R relationship is that hostility emerges finally through frustration experienced by one party because of lack of adjustment by the other. The conflict does not result from change as such, but from the restraints imposed on R by the countries affected. Industrialization or a new philosophy does not cause hostility, but hostility occurs in the first place when resistance is met which limits potential or anticipated developments. It is popularly asserted that all men and nations are instinctively aggressive. Scientifically, "aggression is always a consequence of frustration. . . . The occurrence of aggressive behavior always presupposes the existence of frustration and, contrariwise, the existence of frustration always leads to some form of aggression." [1] Aggression in this sense is defined as behavior which seeks to cause injury to the person toward whom it is directed. The cumulative retaliatory responses which build up once conflict first comes into existence are all aggressive in this sense.

There will be occasions in which resistance to change seems to be desirable, not merely from a national point of view but also from that of the world community. Provision has to be made for appropriate defenses, and this is a matter to which attention will be given. (See Chapter Six.) At the same time, the types of conflict situations outlined in Chapter One suggest that most changes, and certainly most of the changes which have ultimately led

[1] Dollard, J. *et al.*: *Frustration and Aggression* (London: Kegan Paul, Trench, Trubner & Co. Ltd.; 1944), p. 1.

to conflict, are of the primary type—natural or inevitable developments in national life not directed against any other nation. Adjustments by other countries could have led in the long run to a sharing of the gains made possible by the development.

## 2. PRIMARY AND SECONDARY CONTROLS

If conflict emerges from frustration of national ambitions, then controls that are exercised by national or international authorities to prevent change are likely to intensify conflict. The purpose of controls, including the enforcement of decisions of an international authority, is to arrive at the observance of international agreement, or to prevent conflict by a short cut. In other words, international controls seek to prevent war without resolving the conflict. It can be argued, however, that enforcement in fact destroys those conditions necessary for stable peaceful relations and finally creates just the situation it seeks to avoid.

By enforcement is not meant provisions for the peaceful settlement of disputes—conciliation, arbitration, judicial settlement—or even the activities of observers, or the publication of facts and opinions regarding a situation or dispute. By enforcement is not meant inspection systems to ensure that there are no nuclear weapons being tested or produced, nor the exclusion of a nation from a system from which it derives benefits if it no longer wishes to observe the obligations. There is no doubt that in these cases there is an element of enforcement—using national or world public opinion as an agent. By enforcement is meant the causing of frustration by the threat or use of force, by the threat or use of sanctions, by the exclusion of a state from an international society, or by any other barrier to activity to which a sovereign state is not able or likely to adjust itself by passive response.

From this point of view the same classification may be made of controls as was used to differentiate change; there are primary and secondary controls. Primary controls on national policies and actions are the natural environment, including populations, resource development, distance, knowledge, and in addition, other features of the world environment which arise incidentally out of the domestic activities and policies of each state. These primary controls are the static features out of which primary change arises. Secondary controls are those which arise out of the policies and acts of national and international organizations designed to exercise a control on the policies and activities of other nations. Secondary controls include threats of enforcement, procedures associated with national and international defense organizations, and the existence of defense forces, military alliances, and economic blocs.

Indeed, no practical distinction can be made between change and control, except that change could be regarded as alteration in controls. The behaviorist responses are the same whether the activity occurs as a change or is designed as a control. If the intention is deliberately to exercise a restraint or to limit opportunities, there will be a nonpassive response. If there is no intention to frustrate, and the activity is related merely to normal domestic development, there is a greater chance of a passive response.

It follows that if national or international control of aggressive policies takes a form which frustrates even further the ambitions of the revolutionary, it is more likely to provoke increased retaliatory responses than to achieve its purpose. The only restraints or controls upon any nation which are likely to be absorbed, or likely to invite passive response, are limitations imposed by primary controls, that is, limitations which are imposed by the general economic and political environment and not by nations or groups of nations with deliberate and specific intent.

For the most part, primary control comes about by accident. It is wholly objective and impersonal in the sense that no identifiable human agent is discernible. For example, markets determined by world population growth, by reduced demand for goods resulting from the invention of some substitute material, by independence movements over a wide area, by new and independent states, by famine and flood, are controls which exercise limitations on national policies and ambitions and which must be accepted passively. On the other hand, discriminatory trade policies, military and political alliances that exclude countries from normal competition in trade and politics, propaganda monopolies which enable countries to protect themselves against opposing points of view, are among the secondary controls which seek to protect but which actually frustrate and invite new aggressive techniques.

Primary or normal market restrictions on production and on trade, such as droughts, changed demand, and so on, are usually accepted as inevitable. The same quantitative effects brought about by the deliberate policy of another nation cause grave resentment and retaliation. For instance, wheat producers frequently experience grave hardship for climatic reasons, and it is expected by the rest of the community that they should be prepared for this. The loss of markets, however, caused by another

74

producer-country giving surplus wheat to a needy famine area could be a matter of grave international political concern. In the political field, limitations on the pursuit of national interests imposed by the natural distribution of resources or by the stage of their development, are widely accepted. There has been a remarkable acceptance by the Great Powers of the effects of increased membership in the United Nations of smaller powers. The historic inevitability of periods of colonialism seems to be accepted by peoples who win their independence. Indeed, there is a high degree of acceptance of all political forces which appear inevitable in the sense that they are not generated by known and currently identifiable human organizations. On the other hand, restraints imposed on the political and economic development of nations or on their international political and economic relations with others by the threat of force, by regional pacts, or by discriminatory treatment, are not limitations that are accepted passively.

Obviously there cannot be always a clear-cut distinction between primary and secondary controls. There will be many borderline cases, and the degree of objectivity or subjectivity must be considered. For instance, a population growth is a natural development and is not directed against any country. It will nevertheless cause anxiety on the part of neighbors and may provoke defensive responses and aggressive political attitudes. Population growths in Asia must be a major concern to countries placed like Australia and New Zealand, and defensive reactions by them are to be expected. However, if these reactions are in respect to Asian populations generally and not to particular countries, a response by Asian peoples is likely which, if not passive, will at any rate not evoke the intensive aggressiveness which would follow from discrimination against a particular country. In making this classification, the factor of perception is important. A natural development could be erroneously perceived as a restraint deliberately imposed. However, despite the difficulties inherent in any classification of this nature, the concept of differentiation remains not merely useful for analysis but practical. The extremes are clear, and it is not the borderline cases which are important.

The difference in consequence between objective (primary) and subjective (secondary) restraints on nations is of very great practical significance. It touches upon the heart of the problem of international tensions, upon the personality of the power elite, upon human reactions, and upon the elements of prestige and dignity which so often in political life cause reactions to situations out of all proportion to the strength of the stimulus. The identity of the person leading a great national movement is of relatively little importance historically; he can be anyone of many. All national leaders are political persons with similar human reactions. These considerations highlight a fact which much academic study ignores, especially when it tries to make of international relations a science like physics. The problems of international relations are problems of competing human organizations, with competing human power elites, and are, therefore, essentially problems of human reaction—regardless of the particular person who happens to be in effective power at the time.

The practical significance of this is that there is in every case of frustration a strong element of rebellion against outside domination and against restraint. The limitations on national achievement which provoke conflict are not those caused by the weather, or the climate,

76

or scarce resources, or flood, but those imposed by known, identifiable human agents. Every circumstance forced on a nation or on a people by another or by any outside authority is unstable. This is the weakness of the balance of power, of containment, of every endeavor to preserve the status quo. It is the weakness of colonialism and of feudalism. It is the weakness of Communist and non-Communist institutions which are forcibly imposed from without. It is the weakness of international organizations which have power to impose their will. Restraints imposed by an international organization, by agreements entered into under duress, or by the fear of force cannot be more effective than the framework which self-interest erects. The restraints may be effective, at least over the short term. However, a stable condition of peace is possible only where acceptable objective restraints are the only ones in operation.

### 3. THE NATURE OF AGREEMENTS

It is well at this stage to note certain implications inherent in the view that effective enforcement is not possible. Without some means of enforcement, treaties and agreements can never be more than declarations of present intention, to be observed only so long as self-interest requires. Agreeing, for instance, on what constitutes aggression, which is a central issue in international life, is not a problem of human communication or understanding, but a question of intent and of voluntary decision.

The General Assembly's Special Committee on the Definition of Aggression of 1956 failed to produce either a satisfactory definition of "aggression" or a consensus

77

as to the "possibility" or "desirability" of such a definition. The problem was not one merely of human communication. No term is so definite that there cannot be argument concerning its meaning, and no term has meaning unless there is broad agreement on it. The fact is, there is no general agreement as to what constitutes aggression. The attempts by the committee were attempts, in fact, by national representatives to impose that definition which they thought would best serve their own nations' interests. Some nations would argue that even an economic blockade or the nonrecognition of a country constitutes aggression. Certainly both would be included, as intent to damage, in any behaviorist definition of aggression. In practice, however, as long as aggressive policies exist, no definition can be agreed upon, because aggression is part of an over-all situation which makes agreement impossible.

In domestic legislation there is no such urgent need for agreement in the use of terms. Intention is the important thing. Treason, sabotage, espionage, are all subjects on which there is domestic legislation despite the fact that no two people would agree on definition. And yet the intention of the legislation is generally clear, and that intention is carried into effect regardless of difficulties in human communication. Whenever there is an agreed intention, terms and negotiation present few difficulties. Take, for instance, "diplomacy." There is no agreement among nations on a definition which clearly separates acts of diplomacy from other related acts performed by diplomatic representatives, such as the use of propaganda, and of verbal and material persuasion. Yet diplomacy is carried on, and there is a broad general meaning associated with the term which has enabled diplomatic and nondiplomatic activity to be described and formal agreements to be negotiated. It is expedient for governments to have diplomatic representation. "Propaganda" is a term on which the legal representatives of national states would not agree. Yet if governments were to come to the conclusion that it was in their mutual interests to control propaganda, an agreement would soon be reached, and this agreement would carry with it an acceptance and general understanding of the term. There are some hundreds of international agreements. Each one hinges on definition, an acceptance of which is part of the agreement. The inadequacies of human communication are such that terms cannot be defined in any one language without opportunities for dispute, let alone in many languages. Once, however, there is a decision to reach agreement, the agreement itself eliminates argument on terms. If one party wishes no longer to hold to the original agreement, then it can at a later stage place other interpretations upon the terms used, and the agreement becomes inoperative.

Equally, agreements entered into freely will break down once circumstances change—once the intention changes. Agreed amendment might be possible; if not, the agreement ceases to operate. An example is to be seen in the use of the term "regional arrangement" in Chapter VIII of the United Nations Charter. The original intention of the national delegates at San Francisco was quite clear. The dangers of military pacts and power blocs were realized before World War II, and an attempt was made to outlaw them and to substitute regional organization—local Assemblies of debate—which would endeavor to settle regional disputes before they became serious. Chapter VIII provided, among other things, that the "Security Council shall at all times be kept fully informed of activities undertaken or in contemplation under regional arrangements. . . ." Joint power declarations and threats made outside the United Nations seem to be quite inconsistent with the provisions of the Charter. In fact, the Charter envisaged that any combination of powers forming a regional arrangement should include all states within the region, that is, both sides to a dispute, and be used for peaceful settlement of the dispute. No other interpretation can be given to Article 52 as a whole, and in particular to Article 52(2) and (3).[2]

[2] The following is the full text of Chapter VIII. Regional Arrangements.

### Article 52.

1. Nothing in the present Charter precludes the existence of regional arrangements or agencies for dealing with such matters relating to the maintenance of international peace and security as are appropriate for regional action, provided that such arrangements or agencies and their activities are consistent with the Purposes and Principles of the United Nations.

2. The Members of the United Nations entering into such arrangements or constituting such agencies shall make every effort to achieve pacific settlement of local disputes through such regional arrangements or by such regional agencies before referring them to the Security Council.

3. The Security Council shall encourage the development of pacific settlement of local disputes through such regional arrangements or by such regional agencies either on the initiative of the States concerned or by reference from the Security Council.

4. This Article in no way impairs the application of Articles 34 and 35.

### Article 53.

1. The Security Council shall, where appropriate, utilize such regional arrangements or agencies for enforcement action under its authority. But no enforcement action shall be taken under regional arrangements or by regional agencies without the authorization of the Security Council, with the exception of measures against any enemy state, as defined in paragraph 2 of this Article, provided for pur-

However, soon after the San Francisco Conference, the international situation altered, and changes in the concept of regional arrangements became strategically desirable. Regional military pacts, the Atlantic, the Pacific, and the Warsaw Pacts were formed. In no case was the Security Council informed of their activities, and in no case were all relative countries in the region included. It was not difficult to find a plausible justification, and refuge was taken by politicians in Article 51 which states: "Nothing in the present Charter shall impair the inherent right of individual or collective self-defence. . . ." What was not quoted in public statements is the remainder of the same sentence which destroys the refuge: ". . . . *if an armed attack occurs* against a Member of the United Nations, *until* the Security Council has. . . . etc." [3]

---

suant to Article 107 or in regional arrangements directed against renewal of aggressive policy on the part of any such state, until such time as the Organization may, on request of the Governments concerned, be charged with the responsibility for preventing further aggression by such a state.

2. The term enemy state as used in paragraph 1 of this Article applies to any state which during the Second World War has been an enemy of any signatory of the present Charter.

*Article 54.*

The Security Council shall at all times be kept fully informed of activities undertaken or in contemplation under regional arrangements or by regional agencies for the maintenance of international peace and security.

[3] I am aware of the fact that this is a matter which has been debated extensively. Professor Stone (*Legal Controls of International Conflict* [Maitland] 1954 Chapter IX and Discourse 12) has taken the view that NATO and other such organizations are legal in terms of Article 51 as an "escape from the collective security system projected in the Charter." He takes the view that Chapter Eight, Regional Arrangements, does not construct an incompatible alternative to defensive organizations such as NATO. They have a separate function and do not impair in any way

There are, on the other hand, many agreements freely and relatively easily entered into, and the original intention is likely to persist. If the intention is varied by circumstances, amendment is usually as readily agreed to. Examples are agreements governing radio frequencies, postal regulations, navigation, and the many other functional arrangements which govern day-by-day relationships.

These considerations cast doubt on the value of agreements as such. They make the breaking of agreements or attempts to have them amended understandable without recourse to condemnation of the parties concerned. C.Wright Mills has commented: "All nations tend to keep those agreements which their leaders believe it to be advantageous to keep; they tend to break those which their leaders believe put them at a disadvantage." [4]

It follows that international negotiation seeking to establish a condition of peace must work from areas of agreement, and that once in any particular area it is found that agreement is not relatively simple, once it is found that bargaining is required and that an agreed intention cannot be established, further negotiation in such

---

the right of a group of nations to organize *in preparation* for the right to self-defense under Article 51. I think this could be regarded as a legal rationalization of the kind that takes place once nations wish to avoid their obligations. Certainly in the minds of those who took part in the drafting of the Charter, Chapter Eight was designed to make unnecessary, and therefore to prevent, any military arrangements in preparation, which had previously dominated world strategic relations prior to the war. But there was frequently justification by political leaders of NATO and SEATO as being consistent with Chapter Eight. The Charter is now interpreted as allowing strategic groupings which may have a defensive intent, but which equally may have an offensive appearance and effect. The purpose of Chapter Eight was defeated by their existence.

4 Mills, C. Wright: *The Causes of World War Three* (London: Secker and Warburg; 1959), p. 105.

areas should not proceed. Other areas should be explored, and negotiation can return in due course, if agreement still seems desirable, to those areas in which agreement has failed.

When confronted with these realities of Great-Power politics, the Great Powers themselves appreciated this basic nature of international relations. The Security Council rule of unanimity recognized that no decisions could be forced on strong military powers. The assumption was made that if a nation did not happen to be designated at San Francisco as a "Great Power," then enforcement was possible when applied to it. In fact, however, the same resentments are created within a smaller country as would be in a Great Power by any enforced decision which it considers prejudicial to its interests.

One has to look no further than enforced treaties of peace for evidence of this. Either such treaty provisions are ultimately amended, or the defeated nation will itself attempt to break through the restraints imposed upon it. A condition of peace must not rest upon the threatened use of force: not upon deterrents, not upon a balance of power, not upon international forces. A condition of peace, if one is possible at all, must rely upon objectively imposed restraints, and not upon enforcement.

Aside from the problem of enforcement, there remains still another in the creation of a world organization which would be acceptable as decision-making and enforcement body. Experience in the United Nations during the late fifties and early sixties demonstrated that organized voting takes place in a way which leaves the minority with a sense of injustice. This is true, of course, in any local group in which there are voting procedures. In the local group however, there is a greater acceptance of majority decision because there is always the regular opportunity to contest majority control by election processes. There can never be reliable acceptance of majority rule in an international organization.

# 5

The
Self-defeating Nature
of Traditional
Policies and Institutions

## 1. TRADITIONAL THINKING AND INSTITUTIONS

Social theory postulates a gradual extension of social phenomena, including law and order, from the smallest unit, that is, the family or the family tribe, to the state. It was observed by early philosophers that conflict within the tribe was eliminated by tribal leadership and law, and subsequently intertribal conflict was eliminated by the creation of the state. It would appear logical to assume that this associative process would continue until a world order were established in which conflict between states would be eliminated. Indeed, this seems to have been the basis of classical Western thinking. Both Greeks and Romans seem to have looked to a world imperialism in which there would be one sovereign state and a one-world citizenship. The analogy of an extending world order has appeal even in modern times; the concept of "one world" or of "world government" as a means of avoiding war rests upon it. Publicists who advocate such solutions today, however, apparently envisage world government as a voluntary decision by states, unlike the Greeks and Romans who realistically anticipated that it would be possible only by conquest. A nuclear Utopia, in which the victor in nuclear war takes the initiative in creating a universal government, would be consistent with classical thinking. Some interpretations of Communist theory seem also to envisage a centralized world government of socialist units.

If such a world order were possible, it would be logical to argue that those enforcement procedures that ensure peace within a provincial community could be developed within the world community. However, there are both logical and practical reasons for rejecting this evolutionary theory or analogy to provincial government. The reason for the integration of tribes was not merely to enforce intertribal peace, but equally to afford protection of tribes against attack. The expectation of the development of a world order would be logical only if the world were under attack from another planet. There are, furthermore, practical reasons for regarding world government as unreal. There is basic discontinuity between the growth of the state and the further extension of authority to embrace the world. First, cultural and geographic differences, differences in natural resources, differences in political institutions and customs, and other differences among states

86

make any continuity in the process quite unreal. Problems of decentralization in the world arena are different in kind from those in the local environment. At what point the discontinuity occurs, at what size a social unit must be regarded as no longer subject to the techniques and forces operating in the unified community, may be a question for argument; but that there is a point at which unification is not possible is apparent in the modern world. This fact would have been equally clear in the ancient world had early philosophers known about the rest of the world outside Europe and the Middle East.

Secondly, the problems of conquest and of maintenance of law and order by a central authority are quite different in a world community from those in a local state. Psychological and political responses and sentiments of nationalism, racialism, freedom, and independence at once enter into a world society in a way which is incompatible with central control and domination. In retrospect, it is no surprise that events showed Roman imperialism, as a practical military and political procedure, to be impossible of achievement and ultimately unstable even to the limited degree in which it was accomplished. The fate of subsequent imperialisms is likewise understandable. So, too, is the failure of a socialist world to materialize according to the predictions of both Marx and Lenin. It is even more difficult to envisage how a world government would operate in modern times even though it were founded in the wake of a nuclear war, for, assuming the continued existence of organized society, social and economic units would in due course be capable of producing nuclear weapons which would place each of them on a basis of military equality with the central authority.

For all practical purposes it must be assumed that the

basis of world organization is the sovereign state. This has now been widely recognized by political philosophers. St. Pierre, reproducing the *Grand Dessein* of Henry IV, proposed a senate of independent states, and Kant in 1795 set out a scheme for "perpetual peace" which presupposed sovereign states. The League of Nations and the United Nations were both based on the membership of sovereign states.

Although the continued existence of sovereign states has been accepted, the processes and structures put forward for lawmaking and law enforcement have been those which would be appropriate to a theoretical world government. The assumption has been that a valid analogy is to be drawn between local law and order, on the one hand, and on the other, law and order among sovereign states. International forces have been provided, therefore, as a means of ensuring that the principles and decisions of the world body would be observed.

In academic circles and in the popular belief, there are few theories more generally held than that international organization and international control of sovereign states are logically an extension of the processes of national law and order. Quincy Wright asserts: "The role of violence in international law is related to the role of violence in municipal law not only by analogy but also by homology and perhaps by identity." [1] In subsequent chapters he deals with the special problems experienced in international law in terms which indicate that in his view they are problems of growth and evolution, and not difficulties arising out of incompatibility with national law.

[1] A *Study of War* (Chicago: The University of Chicago Press; 1942), Vol. II, p. 874.

Although widely held for many generations, however, the belief that national law will in due course evolve into international law is logically in error. The analogy between national and international law may seem useful to show the kind of development which one might wish to advocate for international relations. But even this is doubtful, since the analogy leads to very misleading speculation. To go further and to argue identity is an error based on the false assumption of the existence of some continuous process commencing with independent sovereign powers and ending in international law and order.

International law employs the same terms as national law; and it is in part this homology which has led to the assumption that the two have some common foundation, and that in due course international enforcement will develop. There is, however, no common foundation; there is no justification even for the use of the same terms. International law, so called, is a purely voluntary observation of codes. It is not law in any sense of the exercise of sovereign powers.

In the national community, law enforcement is applied against a relatively few citizens who might have the desire to break a law. Almost none of these individuals has any final social responsibilities in community decision. They must submit. They have no rights with respect to law breaking. The rights of the individual to freedom of action are regarded by law makers as relatively unimportant compared with the general interests and welfare of the millions who make up the social unit. At best, certain "moral" rights may in some cases be recognized, the exercise of which may lead to alterations in law. In international relations, on the other hand, there are no more than one hundred or so nations, each one of which is acting with full responsibility for its own final decisions and is prepared to defend them as being proper, justifiable, and necessary in the interests of its people. An analogy between two so totally different sets of circumstances is logically not justified.

Any enforcement of international "law" that might take place is, therefore, enforcement by one or more nations in behalf of their own interests and against those of others. It may be that the enforcing group claims to be acting in the interests of the world community, the claim made by democratic government when enforcing law against the private citizen. Equally, the nations against whom enforcement action is taken can claim that they represent the interests of the world community. In practice, however, neither can represent or be regarded as representing "world interests." There is no entirely valid analogy with national law enforcement. The closest resemblance would be found in a national society undergoing political revolution, in which one party endeavors to impose its will upon all others.

There are many major differences between the organization of a state and that of an international system that make analogy of little value. In a state there can be final control of government by the people, usually by election processes. In the international community there is no such control, save war, which it is the purpose of the organization to prevent. International enforcement is a form of tyranny and as such will never be accepted by states against which it is exercised. Again, the national police function has a deliberately deterring effect because it punishes specific crimes. There is no such motivation in international law. There are indeed such things as war crimes, and war trials; and it may be that these are designed for such purpose. In the main, however, international force is used to preserve some interest or to frustrate some ambition, but not to punish on any basis of "accepted law." The "wrongdoer" is that nation which loses in war; the crime is failure to win. The victor becomes the "lawmaker."

The enforcement task of an international organization is performed not by the international organization but by a state or a group of states acting under the jurisdiction of the international body.

When we move over to international legal order all is topsy turvy. Here we have an order not flexible under the hand of a legislator, but held rigid in the grip of States whose joint consent is necessary for change. Here we have, instead of a stability and robustness founded on a public monopoly of force, rather an absence of any substantial public force, and the persistence of great concentrations of military power in the private hands of States. Here at a pinch the public force cannot prevail over the private force wielded by any substantial number of the members of the community; it can attempt at the most to marshal some of these private forces against others, for public ends.[2]

If the purpose of international organization is to provide a first step toward world government in which these problems might be eliminated, then it is self-defeating,

[2] Stone, J.: *Law and Policy in the Quest for Survival.* Australian Broadcasting Commission Lectures, (1960).

for international organization tends to strengthen central-ized governments and administrations. The sociological studies of C.Wright Mills provide strong grounds for thinking that modern governments are not likely either voluntarily to relinquish any powers to a world govern-ment or to be persuaded to do so by public opinion. The traditional view is that the only way in which war be-tween independent nations can be prevented is by the nations' ceasing to be independent. It is unreal, however, to think this will happen. On the contrary, the greater the degree of world organization and co-operation among sovereign states, the greater is the quantity of purely na-tional decision required. In the modern world there are agreements in force covering communications, air safety, trade, and many other operations, but these do not in any way limit national sovereignty. Indeed they strengthen it, because they are effective only by the exercise of such sovereignty. The process of international co-operation strengthens rather than weakens central government and its administrative organs.

As Kant conceded, there can be no voluntary relinquish-ment of sovereignty which includes the relinquishment of enforcement powers. Treaties are binding only so long as it is not in the interests of parties to denounce them. In the more recent terminology of Haas and Whiting:

> If international organizations could exercise a legisla-tive power they would become supranational govern-ments. . . . Such a power, however, does not exist. The only approximation to legislation is the ability to prepare draft treaties, which may become part of the domestic law of the member states—if they

choose to ratify. In essence, therefore, international organizations can only propose laws to their members but not make them. . . . But to the extent that member states voluntarily bind themselves by accepting the treaties and rules drafted by these agencies, what can be done to enforce the obligations? True, the violator of a sanitary or postal convention can be sued before the International Court of Justice. But that tribunal, in turn, is powerless to enforce its decision. Is there a parallel to the policeman of the national community who can bring about compliance? . . . Clearly, the efficacy of international organization does not derive from any powers analogous to those of national governments.[3]

One practical objection to the theory of an expanding legal process relates specifically to the nuclear age. The problem is no longer one of merely reducing the frequency of war; it has become imperative to eliminate war of all kinds, for fear that even a limited war could result in the use of large nuclear weapons. Even if world government of sovereign states were possible by peaceful means, the time required in process would rule it out as a practical procedure in modern conditions.

## 2. OUTMODED TRADITIONAL STRUCTURES

Erroneous views on the nature of social evolution, and the false expectation that there would be a relinquishment of sovereignty, led to policies and structures which could not even in theory achieve the results sought. Na-

[3] *Dynamics of International Relations* (New York: McGraw-Hill Book Co.; 1956), pp. 439-40.

93

tional policies of defense were not effective in preventing war, nor in controlling change. The League of Nations did not develop toward world government, nor has the United Nations. At best, these traditional policies and structures have had a relevance in the sense that tribal warfare once had a relevance to social organization—the defense of national interests by force and through international alliances is a stage through which world society has had to pass.

The projection of these sociological views and of the related policies and institutions into the second half of the twentieth century was not merely false in basic reasoning but also irrelevant to the circumstances. The main features of world society after the forties were as follows:

a. There was a tendency for disputes to be related more to internal social organization, welfare, freedoms, and cultural developments, than to discovery of new territories or to changes in boundaries (except where they became involved in ideological dispute).

b. Available to many nations, even in a condition of disarmament, were nuclear and other weapons of mass destruction, making impractical even limited warfare between nations, and ruling out international enforcement by any group of nations.

c. Demands for change and for social justice were heeded and acted upon in many countries. Social advances resulted from the work of nineteenth-century political philosophers, from the opportunities afforded to independence movements during World War II, and from the nuclear stalemate which forced reconsideration of domestic and foreign policies in the main states.

94

d. There was increased political interest in and knowledge of the effects of frustration, not merely within
small social units but also within the world community.

e. Improvements took place in communication which
promoted the flow of new ideas, and therefore increased the rate of change and the speed with which
conflict could both develop and be resolved.

All these features were interrelated. The nuclear stalemate provided opportunities for integration through conflict, gave time for adjustment, and forced a reconsideration of ideological as well as of military positions. The
acceptance of the inevitability of change, and a willingness on the part of governments to adjust their peoples
to it, were also affected by the nuclear threat, and this in
turn helped to facilitate integration through conflict.
Knowledge and communications led to a greater understanding of motivations, of new ideas, and of the living
conditions of peoples who had been isolated from the rest
of the world. The combined result of all these factors
created a situation wholly different from that which prevailed even at the beginning of the century. The nature
of conflict and the size of weapons were wholly different,
and the degree of acceptance of change and of knowledge
regarding social organization were of an order which made
them, for practical purposes, different in kind.

Those international political institutions which had
been handed down from previous centuries, such as balance of power and other concepts of enforcement seeking
to maintain a status quo, were outmoded by the nuclear
deterrent. Attempts to adjust them or to reconstitute
them within the framework of the nuclear threat were

95

doomed to failure. For instance, the "limited war" policy advocated by some was an attempt to reinstate within the framework of the nuclear deterrent those means for the prevention of change which the nuclear deterrent had rendered inoperative. Even without the nuclear deterrent traditional institutions were outmoded; changes in political values, in ideologies, in concepts of independence and sovereign integrity, had made them irrelevant to the modern world.

There was in the fifties an inherent incompatibility and inconsistency in Western political thinking, leading to major differences in views and to indecision on policies. On the one hand, the traditional conception of statecraft prevailed, and the assumption of aggressive tendencies on the part of states counselled the need for traditional means of defense and alliances. On the other hand, change and its acceptance as being just and inevitable were not reflected in the development of any procedures to facilitate it. The traditional structures inhibited change. There was no synthesis; conflict still developed over changes which in fact were politically acceptable, and to which nations could have made adequate adjustments. In 1960-1 the fighting in Laos seemed to reflect this conflict in Western thinking—the inevitability of changes in government from pro-Western to at least "neutral" had been accepted, yet the military alliance of SEATO was used as a threat against even this change. Much of the aggression of past ages was promoted by demands for justice which were not then recognized. In the modern world such demands are recognized as representing an inevitable stage of development to which adjustment should be made; but no accompanying adaptation of structures has taken place.

It should be noted in passing that a growing acceptance of change in social organization in response to demands for justice is no less significant in relation to internal conflict, to which Marx paid attention, than to international disputes, which were Hegel's concern. Changes in attitudes are likely to permit change in domestic class relationships just as freely as they permit change in relationships between colonial powers and colonial peoples. Indeed, the two processes are likely to proceed together. The predictions of Marx may, moreover, be no less outmoded by sociological development in capitalist countries, by the acceptance of change, by the growth of concepts of social justice, than they have been by the invention of nuclear weapons. This is an observation which did not escape the notice of Soviet leaders in the late fifties.

We have argued that human society is arriving at a stage which can be characterized as follows:

a. Conflict, or at least a great proportion of conflict, is recognized as being due to frustration and to a sense of injustice, rather than to unreasonable or "natural" tendencies toward aggression and fighting for its own sake.

b. There are intellectually, if not always in practice, an understanding and acceptance of claims by other nations based on justice, racial equality, and related concepts. In this respect, our age diverges from earlier political thought.

c. The structures and processes of national and world organization, evolved originally to preserve the status quo, tend to inhibit change even when the change itself appears to be politically acceptable.

d. Nuclear weapons have made the full employment of these structures and processes impracticable; and so-

ciological insight has made them irrelevant and undesirable as a means of achieving peaceful international relations.

e. There is, nevertheless, a lack of development of relevant processes of change, and an absence of synthesis
between structures and sociological thinking.

A behaviorist approach to international relations tends
to emphasize the inevitability of change, the need for adjustments to change, and the necessity for processes and
structures which do not frustrate change but facilitate
the adjustment to it. It tends to challenge the structures
in national and international society which seek to maintain given strategic or other positions by means of power
balances or deterrents. According to the traditional concept of sovereignty, each nation has a right to determine
its own policies and to protect its own interests, regardless
of the effects upon others. There can be no denial of
this right in a world comprising independent sovereign
states. When this right is exercised without consideration
of the responses of others, however, there is likely to arise
a situation of conflict in which the interests to be protected, and others as well, are actually destroyed. The
whole concept of national defense against the normal
competitive activities of others, and the whole structure
of international organization, including power alliances
and power balances which seek to maintain the status quo,
run counter both to behaviorist considerations and to the
circumstances of the nuclear age.

In fact, it could be argued that the greatest potential
source of open warfare in the modern world is the persistence of policies and structures traditionally employed
to prevent the emergence of conflict, and to prevent con-

flict from being resolved in the course of normal competitive activities between nations. Such policies and structures, founded on false expectations of an expanding social organization, are both irrelevant to modern conditions and self-defeating.

# 6

###### ❧❧❧❧❧

# National Policies
# in a
# Condition of Peace

## 1. A CONDITION OF PEACE

We have argued that primary change tends to provoke response or secondary change which is defensive in character and provocative of still further reactions. The behaviorist approach to international relations suggests, therefore, that direct action is not an effective defense against change; because any response which is retaliatory in nature and which does not *absorb* change, is extremely unlikely to inhibit it, but tends rather to start a chain reaction of nonpassive responses ending in open conflict.

Passive response by any nation to limitations imposed by identifiable social organizations is, nevertheless, most unlikely. Secondary change, even in the twentieth century, has been almost always a direct response, a counteraction, a retaliatory move, a political isolation, or even a military threat aimed directly against some nation in which original change took place. Competitive subsidies, competitive alteration of exchange rates, competitive rearmament, and retaliatory restriction on diplomatic rights and on the movements of citizens have been typical.

The problem of secondary change is, therefore, a fundamental one. Conflict can still occur even where there is a high degree of adjustment passively made, where there is a high degree of perception of that adjustment by the other power, and where there is a high degree of mutual assistance and co-operation to ensure that change and adjustment create as little disturbance as possible. The capacity of any system to absorb change, especially political change, is greatly limited. In some cases total absorption would mean the destruction of an important industry, or the acceptance of a competing ideology or economic system. For this reason "one world" or "world imperialism" is not a practicable possibility, because nations will always try to preserve those institutions and attitudes they believe to be of value. The mere existence of cultural, economic, and political differences among states limits the capacity to absorb change. They are as vital as boundary lines.

There must be some kind of national defense against any change which in the view of people concerned would destroy essential interests. The problem is, then, to ascertain what defensive responses are possible, what secondary changes are possible, which do not in the real world lead to still other defensive responses. The relationship between S and R is inherently unstable. There can never be a completely peaceful relationship. We have already stated that the concept of "One World" is impossible. We have to ascertain, therefore, what types of defensive response can lead partly to absorption and partly to defense and engender the least possible further reaction. Political policies in the post-World War II period brought about cumulative responses which achieved just the opposite results from those desired, as do contractions in credit in times of recession. We have to ascertain those policies which, without endangering security, bring about cumulative processes in the opposite direction, as does credit expansion in times of recession.

In other words, war can be avoided and a condition of peace established only if there can be found effective defensive or protective responses to which in turn there will be only passive responses. A condition of peace is not some unstable S/R relationship maintained by force, a balance of power, or a deterrent. It is a condition of peaceful relationship brought about partly by absorption of change and partly by defensive policies which invite only passive responses.

## 2. PEACE AS A FUNCTION OF NATIONAL POLICIES

If passive responses could be found which would afford adequate protection of vital interests, it would become a matter of free choice on the part of governments whether they promote or destroy a condition of peace, just as it is a matter of deliberate choice for governments whether they create conditions of inflation or of unemployment. If passive responses could be determined, governments would have a knowledge of permissible defenses and a clear insight into the consequences of their policies.

We are making the assumption that given a choice between responses provocative of retaliation and those not so, governments would adopt passive ones, provided the latter accomplished satisfactorily their protective objectives. This is a reasonable assumption. Repression of the unemployed was the basis of policy only because no other was known. Plague and disease were dealt with by witchcraft only because bacteria and medical science had not provided alternatives. In international relations defense responses are employed, such as discriminatory tariffs, armaments, alliances, political isolation, and propaganda, even though they evoke further reactions and a cumulative situation, only because no other policies are known and because the practical consequences of the usual ones are not clear.

The task of political science, therefore, in relation to the prevention of conflict, is to find the defensive responses which do not lead to cumulative reactions, and which at the same time reasonably protect the institutions and interests of nations by allowing time for those mutual adjustments which, in due course, may seem to be desirable. Conciliation, arbitration, diplomatic negotiations, adjustment processes, and many other features of international relations are relevant and important in time of conflict. They are, however, ancillary to passive responses, or more precisely, they become relevant only after conflict has developed, after there have been responses and reactions of an aggressive nature. The problem of peaceful international relations is to ascertain those responses and circumstances which do not permit conflict to develop, and which always allow the potentially unstable S/R relationship to continue as a stable condition of absorption and adjustment.

Described in these terms, the problem of peaceful

international relations is a problem of national policies, and not of international organization. We have observed that if the potentially unstable S/R relationship is held stable by some outside force, it is likely, quite suddenly, to appear as an advanced stage of conflict. Foreign restraints, even international ones, tend to promote instability. The passive response has to be of such a character that it provides for the defense of S, or for restraints upon R, by an objective (primary) and not a subjective (secondary) force.

### 3. THE PRINCIPLE OF NONDISCRIMINATION

The search is, therefore, for those national policies which avoid retaliatory responses. A feature of the period preceding World War II was economic discrimination; the reserving of colonial markets for the trade of the metropolitan powers, discriminatory quotas, economic blocs, all contributed to the pattern of discriminatory international trading relations. Indeed, as we have argued, it was the existence of this pattern which brought into play those forces that ultimately led Japan into war against the West, and which contributed to the economic conditions of Germany that paved the way for military dictatorship. This was recognized in the postwar reconstruction period; an effort was made to eliminate discrimination by postwar reconstruction planning and negotiation. Nondiscrimination became probably the most universally accepted principle in international commercial relations. One example of this was the widespread operation of the most-favored-nation principle. It was written into the General Agreement on Tariffs and Trade and became a part of most multilateral agreements.

It was practical experience in commercial dealings, and the evidence of political repercussions from discriminatory trading practices, which led to this almost universal acceptance of nondiscrimination. A theoretical behaviorist approach leads to the same conclusion. It follows from the observations made in Chapter Four regarding subjective and objective restraints on national development, that market changes—for instance a change in consumption habits, or even the introduction of substitute materials—would be tolerated as a natural and inevitable development, carrying with it no aggressive motivation, even though the main center of change were identifiable. There would tend to be passive responses and an absorption of change by transfers to other industries, by increased advertising, by research into new uses and new markets, and so on. On the other hand, a less damaging alteration in markets, caused by the deliberate policy of a government to prejudice some other particular source because of low costs, political environment, or some other such reason, would be a change to which there would be no passive response. Retaliation in some form could be expected. However, the principle of nonenforcement or objectivity in control was not yet recognized as such. It was commercial experience, rather than any understanding of the behaviorist reactions to discrimination, which led to nondiscriminatory commercial policies after World War II. Consequently, the principle of nondiscrimination was not given general application. It was not applied to international relations outside the realm of commerce.

Evidence of this is in the Charter of the United Nations. While principles of sovereign equality and human rights without distinction as to race, sex, language, or religion were spelt out and were included in several different contexts, nowhere in the Charter was there any reference to nondiscrimination as a national policy. Furthermore, the Charter of the United Nations was based on the principle of enforcement, which, as we have argued, implies in international relations discrimination against certain sovereign states by others. It is noteworthy that Wright in his *Study of War* recognizes nondiscrimination only with respect to commercial dealings (except in the limited context of neutrality).

Soon after the Charter conference of 1945, the S/R conflict between the West and the Communist powers took a form quite different from the prewar economic conflict between the West and Germany. The conflict of ideologies was now more important than any struggle for markets. Political discrimination was as important as an instrument of national policy as had been economic discrimination in the prewar period. Barriers to political contact from the outside, internal repression or discouragement of foreign philosophies, the gradual forming of political blocs based on the acceptance of ideologies rather than on the advantages of trading, led to a situation in which political and strategic organizations dominated international relations. Political discrimination was the outstanding feature of all foreign strategic policies, affecting economic aid, propaganda, diplomatic relations, and all relations outside commercial relations, and affecting even these when political considerations overrode commercial interests. The only exceptions were to be found in the policies of some small powers which endeavored to conduct their relations on a basis of neutralism.

It was only in the late fifties that the cumulative effects of political discrimination became apparent. Insofar as governments sought to avoid them, it was for pragmatic reasons, and not because of any understanding as yet of the theoretical effects of discrimination. Nonrecognition of China by the United States and other countries began to be recognized as futile. It caused no embarrassment to Communist China, for she was indeed able still to trade and to carry on relations with most of the world just the same. On the contrary, the policy of nonrecognition was generating sympathy for her among Asian countries, instead of discouraging their support. Furthermore, the isolation from normal contact, while not bringing any strategic benefits, was actually creating a situation of increasing suspicion and distrust. What amounts to a controlled experiment in discriminatory foreign policy was available for observation in the fifties. Russia, the leading Communist country, the originator of the S/R conflict, was formally recognized by and in close touch with Western powers. Conflict integration was perceptible as a result of many negotiations, private and official. Tourists and commercial visitors maintained contact despite high political tension. Extensive contact was being made between scientists and official advisers of Russia and the United States. At the same time, the Communist government in China was isolated. Contacts were reduced to a minimum and almost eliminated in so far as United States citizens were concerned. The result was ignorance on both sides, no conflict integration, no reliable knowledge of either side by the other. From the nature of past trading and political associations, and in view of the general attitudes in the West towards China and Russia, far better relations could have been expected with a Communist China than with a Communist Russia had there been the same contact.

During the same period it began to be clear that regional defense organizations such as the South East Asia Treaty Organization, which were discriminatory in character and sought to restrain particular countries, did not win the support of important countries in the area, did not achieve their purposes, and merely aggravated already existing tensions between the West and the Communist countries.

Political preference goes primarily according to strategic and military preference, but this means preference in the supply of equipment and capital. Conditions are thus created, including commercial privileges, which are heavily discriminatory. It is quite impossible to separate political from commercial discrimination. This was at the basis of much of the tension between Asian and Western countries in the fifties. Ceylon, India, and other Asian countries who traded on a nondiscriminatory basis with China, with whom they maintained also diplomatic relations, were thought by the United States to be undermining Western strategic policies.

Although at the present writing it may be too early to know, it would appear that by 1960 there was a growing pragmatic realization among political leaders of all the main countries of the futility and dangers of political discrimination, just as there had been at the end of the previous war of economic discrimination. Still the feeling was pragmatic. There was as yet no acceptance of a theory, and there were no accepted principles which could guide policy. If political and economic discrimination seemed to be in the interests of national expediency, then there was no known reason of principle for not adopting either or both. It is, however, necessary, in order to reduce political tension, that there be general acceptance of the principle of nondiscrimination, as the basis for an international policy of nonenforcement and objective control. It has been abundantly demonstrated in recent political experience and needs now to be recognized as a behaviorist principle, that discrimination invariably induces frustration and aggressive response.

Examples of discriminatory defense and of alternative nondiscriminatory defense will help to make the argument clear. When R alters international trading relations by coming into the market with goods produced by cheap labor, S, a relatively high-cost producer and also an importer of the same goods, can impose quotas and restrict the entry from the low-cost producer while leaving high-cost producers unaffected. This was, of course, the position India faced during the industrial revolution in Britain, and which Japan faced before World War II. The alternative is to raise all duties so that the domestic producer obtains the required protection, and so that the balance of the home market is shared by all foreign suppliers in competitive conditions. This was, after the war, an accepted procedure. Import quotas, licensing, and exchange control can be administered so as to discriminate; but, generally speaking, after World War II all such practices that were brought to light were regarded as being contrary to the accepted codes of the period.

The composition of a nation's population and the nature of its migration policy generally are held to be matters of domestic jurisdiction. A government may limit inflow in many ways. Quotas are essentially discriminatory unless based on some mathematical proportions which give as much opportunity to nationals of one nation as to those of others. This would in most cases, of course, defeat their purpose. A government can maintain its population composition by excluding peoples of certain races, cultures, or ideologies. In due course, however, this must cause resentment, frustration, and aggressive behavior, even though the peoples discriminated against have no desire to migrate. A similar objective can be achieved by nondiscriminatory means—for instance, by an insistence on generally applicable standards of health, of education, and even of capital resources—all of which are relevant and acceptable restrictions and which could apply to all peoples and countries equally without arbitrary and discriminatory judgment. This procedure could prevent the influx of nonassimilable peoples of low living standard.

The encouragement of capital from some sources and not from others, the entry of publications from some nations and not from others, travel restrictions in some areas and not in others, are examples of the kind of discriminatory policies which, whether or not they achieve their avowed strategic objectives, create conditions of cumulative reaction. The security objective is probably best achieved in politically advanced countries by the greatest possible freedom to study all competing ideologies. In less advanced countries the free discussion of alternative forms of governments is the only process by which relevant institutions can develop. In times of swift transport and instantaneous communication, it is impossible to isolate any people permanently and completely from external ideas, and the attempt to do so merely creates the kind of internal frustration and unrest which the isolation is designed to avoid.

At this point, however, there enter questions of defense and internal security which are by their nature discriminatory. The application of nondiscrimination in this field is a contradiction in terms. It is to be noted, however, that there can be degrees of discrimination in defense. For instance, in a world in which there were a true balance of power, in which all nations were more or less equal in power, defense of any one nation would be conducted on a nondiscriminatory basis. In the real world there are countries, especially small ones, that have defense forces without any particular orientation; they are not directed more against one country than another. The cumulative effects of competitive defense are then reduced to a minimum. Once, however, conflict develops to the stage where defense is oriented against some particular power, once bases, specialized weapons, and procedures direct defense against a particular country, then immediately there is likely to be an intensive arms race. A useful first step in disarmament in a situation of high political tension would probably be the introduction of increasing degrees of nondiscrimination by the removal of weapons and establishments which are specifically oriented.

### 4. INDEPENDENCE AND NONINTERVENTION

A corollary of nondiscrimination is nonintervention in the affairs of other states, and full observance of national independence. There is strong popular appeal, of course, in being independent, but the significance of national independence from an international point of view lies in its relevance to the maintaining of peace. If there is not complete independence, if one state exercises political or economic control over another to its own advantage, the conditions of objective control and nondiscrimination are destroyed and subjective or secondary controls are imposed on third parties. The most obvious example is the case in which one major power influences the economic and foreign policies of smaller states in such a way that there is formed a power bloc which employs its combined economic and military strength and its combined voting strength to limit the competitive success of third parties. Blocs are obvious in their operations. The same subjective control is produced in varying degrees by any bilateral or multilateral actions which prejudice the free competitive position of other nations.

It should be noted in passing that this observation does not carry with it any suggestion that governments are likely voluntarily to avoid exercising an influence on other states. The conditioning of the international environment to discourage this form of discrimination is a matter for later examination. We are concerned at the moment merely to record the features of national policies which appear to be part of a theoretical condition of peace.

A distinction can be made usefully between the exercise of an effective influence, on the one hand, which follows without any deliberate intent from commercial relations and cultural ties, and the exercise, on the other, of an effective influence resulting from deliberate political and strategic policies. In a world of very great and very small nations, in a world divided into nations and regions of different racial and cultural groups, in a world in which there are states with common regional and commercial interest, there are bound to be groupings, and in this sense, forms of discrimination. These groupings and natural sympathies must be classified, along with the existence of states and of other primary conditions, as part of the objective environment in which national policies operate. As such they would not impose subjective or secondary restraints upon other nations. In practice they are so classified. Relationships within the British Commonwealth are based on traditional and cultural ties, and out of this relationship flow many advantages of consultation and even of trade. They do not cause frustration or aggressive responses, provided, at least, they remain of this character and do not constitute an organized bloc to obtain advantage at the expense of other nations. During the thirties, however, the Commonwealth relationship included discriminatory preferences, causing much resentment, especially in the United States because of its ties with Canada, and resulting in aggressive responses and every attempt to break the Imperial Preferences system. European Union or a common-market scheme would similarly be accepted by other nations as a natural development, and not intentionally directed against their interests, if it sought no discriminatory advantages and acted as a unified state. Consultations among Communist countries and discussions of their common problems are not a cause of frustration and aggressive responses by the West any more than are Western consultations on fiscal policies, provided, of course, that the final result of these conferences is not the adoption of policies designed to prejudice the interests of other countries. Similarly, regional arrangements under Chapter VIII of the Charter of the United Nations would be regarded by all nations not in the region as being a nondiscriminatory means of solving regional problems, and not as being directed against any particular nation or group of nations.

On the other hand, deliberate discrimination by a nation or a group of nations, intended to damage the interests of another nation or group of nations, evokes aggressive responses. Examples are the trade embargoes and restrictions by the West against Communist countries, the exclusion by Communist countries of publications and broadcasts from the West, regional security pacts, and discriminatory economic aid.

While there are many examples both of natural (primary) and of deliberate (secondary) influence by some powers over the affairs of others, there are also very many cases in which it would be difficult to determine whether the primary or the secondary motivations were predominant. For instance, during the fifties many smaller Western countries lost some of their independence in foreign policy to the United States. In some respects this was a natural development arising out of common cultural and economic interests, and a traditional desire to keep in step with another country with a similar background. In other respects it was a development deliberately arranged, for reasons of security on the part of the smaller countries and for trading and investment advantage on the part of the United States.

The interaction of primary and secondary influence over other nations by great powers in the power-bloc situation of the late fifties led to a bipolarization in which all nations were strategically grouped about the two main powers, with the exception of a few Asian nations, notably India, Ceylon, and Indonesia, which attempted to avoid alignment. In these circumstances even the natural links among nations became suspect, losing their objective quality. The traditional relations existing between the United States and the Latin American states appeared more and more to the Communist countries as a deliberate denial to them of a large part of the world economy and political society. On the other hand, the natural affiliation among Communist countries appeared similarly to the United States. As some of these affiliations were confirmed by military ties, there was good reason for perception of them as secondary change.

Once there is bipolarization in the international world, smaller nations, especially those with governments not confident of their own popular support, tend to seek protection against revolt from the power in whose orbit they lie. The influence of the great power then becomes virtual control. It determines the government of the satellite and protects it until its power elite can sustain itself. The satellite becomes a strategic asset of the great power, and as such it becomes a factor in the subjective control being exercised upon the other power bloc. Any sign of internal unrest invites attempts by the opposing power bloc to undermine the protected government and to bring about change.

Once there is political interest in the internal affairs of one country by another, once change in the internal affairs of any country becomes a matter of strategic concern to others, independence is destroyed. If the government of one independent nation can seek and obtain the support of another nation, it means that alignments, discriminations, and competition in military power are taking place, and the condition of peace is destroyed.

This was, in fact, the position after World War II. Internal unrest in countries of strategic importance to one bloc or the other was frequently attributed to foreign intervention by countries having different political institutions. Attempts to maintain the status quo were attributed to countries having similar political institutions. During this period there was no greater source of tension than the protection by foreign governments of administrations which were not, for one reason or another, able to command internal support sufficient to counter rebellion.

Where direct intervention was not possible, economic and military aid was directed to the support of governments which needed political assistance. When these forms of nonmilitary aggression failed to subvert or to maintain, whichever was the object, and where the country was of strategic importance, force and the threat of force were employed. Colonial and feudal administrations in South East Asia, the Middle East, and elsewhere, were maintained by the West as part of a defensive reaction against the spread of communism. Communist governments gave economic and military support to Communist movements and to Communist governments in Hungary, Poland, and underdeveloped areas in which political conflict was being waged.

The justification for the use of force lay in the claim that change was in fact being brought about, or alternatively that change which would normally have occurred was being prevented, not by the will of the people in the country concerned but by a foreign power. Either the "legitimate" government was being defended at its own request, or alternatively, the people were being helped to overthrow the existing ("legitimate") government which had no right of existence because of its tyranny.

The principle of nondiscrimination would debar any external interference in the operation of national government. Under this principle any government would be free to maintain itself and to prevent internal political change by any means at its disposal. It could create barriers between its country and the outside world; it could restrict foreign visitors, business men, and diplomats; it could try to prevent outside propaganda; and it could employ repression. This is the way in which a modern state with a strong power elite does in fact operate. These are matters

116

of domestic jurisdiction. It is unlikely that internal repression could do more than postpone internal change. If there were no intervention from outside, any government meeting with internal opposition it could not withstand would fall. There could not be outside intervention in the internal affairs of any country, even at the request of a "legitimate" government. The "legitimate" government would be no more legitimate than its internal support made it. The "de facto" government, and not the "de jure" government, is the only legitimate government in a condition of peace.

Consequently, a condition of international peace by definition includes political change within national boundaries, either by peaceful means, by *coup d'état*, or by revolution. By these processes national unity and cohesion are at times achieved. A condition of international peace includes revolts against tyranny, against feudalism in all its forms, against any form of repression, against any form of government or administration thought by others to be good or bad. Put in another way, a behaviorist concept of a condition of international peace allows that political change and development should take place even in conditions where that change is possible only by violence. This same consideration applies to the position of dependent and subjugated peoples. The concept of a condition of peace includes internal conflict where people effectively demand freedom and self-determination which is being denied them. Assistance from other nations destroys the conditions of nondiscrimination, and invites responses from still other nations.

Another example of the same proposition is the case in which there is external domination not of a nation directly but of minorities or majorities within the nation affecting

117

the freedom and independence of the nation as a whole. For instance, domination of political or of religious groups from a foreign country must in due course divide the nation concerned and lead to conflict and to the ultimate overthrow of its government or its institutions. Such internal conflict, whether peaceful or violent, is not incompatible with a behaviorist concept of international peace so long as there is no outside attempt to interfere.

This does not, of course, necessarily justify internal strife in any country at any stage of its political development. There will be those who will argue that no long-term benefit can be gained by violent revolution, and that passive resistance is the only appropriate response to unpopular government. Whether this be so is not a matter which comes into consideration in the behaviorist study of a condition of international peace. In order for there to be international peace based on nondiscrimination, there must be freedom of political development within any national unit. Where the process of internal national development raises moral or philosophic issues, they are quite outside the scope of this study.

### 5. DOMESTIC JURISDICTION

The principle of domestic jurisdiction in this context is important. The principle was included in the Charter of the United Nations to protect rights over migration policies and other policies which might be attacked on the international forum. In the view of those who look forward to the gradual extension of national law to international law and organization, the observance of this principle is a barrier to future development. In the view we have adopted—that there can be no extension from the national to the international society—strict observance of domestic jurisdiction is important. Any interference by an outside authority with the decisions of a state is first an act of discrimination, seeking an advantage at the expense of that state or of some other; and secondly, it is a frustration of the aims of the nation interfered with, or of significant sections of it, leading to conflict.

The intervention by the West into Russian affairs after World War I and into Chinese affairs after World War II both demonstrate the reactions which can be expected to outside attempts to control or to influence the internal affairs of a nation. The intervention of the United Nations into Congo affairs in 1960 could have been justified only on the basis of maintaining law and order and of the disarming of all forces. There was, however, interference into matters essentially of domestic jurisdiction, which is not open to any nation, not even the United Nations, and not even at the request of the current head of state. The concept of "legitimate" government has no place in a condition of international peace, whether invoked by a nation or by an international authority. The division of Germany and of Korea were likewise instances of intervention into domestic jurisdiction, the victors having failed to disarm these countries and to leave them to work out their own future.

It follows that the development of stable political institutions and strong political leadership in new independent nations would make a contribution to a condition of peace. This is the relevance of economic and technical aid, and of research into political institutions appropriate for newly developed nations.

In Europe during the thirties new methods of economic penetration were invented. Germany was able to destroy national independence in other countries without relying upon political techniques or upon the weapons of subversion developed after World War II. The period between the two wars was one of intense research by political scientists into new trading techniques and their political effects. After World War II, and as a result of knowledge gained and agreements reached, economic penetration played a minor role. From an economic point of view, there appeared to be no important factors present in the real world which would upset a condition of peace. Political forms of penetration were being examined by organizations such as SEATO in the fifties, but there was no international discussion on them or on agreements providing for their control. From a political point of view, the world had features of political and strategic competition involving small nations which could destroy a condition of peace, just as previously national economic policies destroyed economic co-operation.

### 6. THE CONTROL OF SECONDARY CHANGE

Several conclusions emerge. A condition of peace would be assisted if national policies were deliberately conceived to encourage community acceptance of change, and to encourage passive responses to conditions objectively imposed. A changed productive technique in a particular foreign country resulting in competition in the national market should be met not by a discriminatory tariff but by deliberate policies of capital transfer and the provision of alternate employment opportunities, or alternatively by policies of protection which are not discriminatory. The introduction into political thought of a new philosophy should be met not by censorship and the suppression of political parties but by deliberate policies calculated to encourage discussion and consideration of new ideas.

Public acknowledgment of adjustments which have been made to change would assist perception by opposing powers and would tend to have the effect of delaying nonpassive reactions. But there are difficulties in doing this. In R countries (for instance Communist countries), adjustments or deviations from a predetermined course are difficult to make, and cannot easily be admitted even when made. In S countries (for instance Western countries), it is politically difficult to admit to a change in attitude or policy, or to a compromise, or to an accommodation of a new idea which comes from the R country against which defensive action is being taken. Adjustment is, politically, something to hide; whereas in theory it is something to publicize as a basic contribution to a condition of peace of which a national could be proud.

Despite the responsibilities of S, a passive response is not solely a function of S. It is in the interests of R that the adjustments should be made, so that there can be a full exploitation of the change. It is in the interests of R, therefore, in so far as is possible, to assist in making adjustments smooth and practicable. This can be done by control of the change, by advice of its likelihood, by the initiation of other changes which would be to the advantage of S, and so on. International discussion on probable population changes, resource development, centralized programs of development, changes in educational systems, and research of many kinds, are all relevant in this context. The policy of rival governments during the fifties was to try to embarrass each other. The Western hope and aim were to inspire internal unrest within the Communist countries; and the Communist hope and aim were to see the quickest possible deterioration of the capitalist system. For the sake of peaceful relationships, the policy of both should probably have been to assist each other, the Communist to maintain political stability and the capitalist to maintain economic stability so that the S/R relationship could remain stable, thus permitting of progressive changes and adaptations which could be absorbed.

### 7. A CONDITION OF PEACE IS NOT SELF-SUPPORTING

A theoretical concept of a condition of peace is one in which each nation pursues its own national aims in conformity with a universal policy objectively imposed. This universal policy is dictated by each nation's knowledge of the effects of its own policies on other nations, and by the necessity of avoiding policies which prejudice the interests of other nations and which invite defensive and retaliatory reactions. Each nation acting independently can satisfy its international objectives, economic, social, and political, in ways which afford each nation equal marginal satisfactions. Each nation considers it is achieving its aims to the maximum degree possible, having in mind the competing aims of others. In actual practice, while no nation is ever complacent about its success in foreign commercial relations, there is very generally an acceptance of the limitations on possible success. Indeed, governments never cease to boast of their achievements in international competition. Unless there are specific barriers which they are attempting to break down, they express satisfaction with the position within the existing market conditions, that is within the structure established by the competing interests of others.

After World War II there developed in the field of economic and trading relations a significant body of agreement amounting to a code of national behavior. This experience suggests that once nations have knowledge of the ways in which their interests can best be pursued, of the reactions of other nations whose interests might be threatened, of the reactions of others who are not on this occasion threatened but who might be in some future case, there is automatically a self-control more powerful than that which could be exercised by any outside force or controlling body.

However, the true independence and freedom of smaller nations will not be rendered secure *by the mere agreement of Great Powers not to interfere*—because their strategic and economic competition will lead them to interfere as much as they can unless they perceive clearly the ultimate consequences. Nor can this independence of smaller nations be achieved by the two rival powers' *preventing each other* from interfering. They have tried to do this, not in the interests of the independence of the smaller states but in their own strategic interests. This is a source of "limited" wars. The independence of the smaller nations is not then being protected; nation states are being fought over, and the prize is their allegiance.

Clearly knowledge and experience alone are not sufficient to ensure peace in the real world. The level of knowledge within the power elite, and the state of conventional wisdom, fall far short of the requirements of peaceful international relations. In the absence of clear knowledge of self-interest and a widespread understanding of it, all manner of self-interests, even narrower than the national, enter into policy-making, with disastrous results from the point of view of a condition of peace. This does not destroy the concept of international peace. It merely underlines the need for greater knowledge regarding the basis of peaceful relationship. It underlines the need, also, for some conditioning of national policies to ensure their conformity with the requirements of a condition of peace. It is to this we now turn.

# 7

## The Conditioning of National Policies

### 1. SUMMARY OF ANALYSIS

We have arrived, then, at this position. Competition between sovereign states is a normal condition, and conflict arises out of it as a result of nonpassive responses to change. World government, or a universal imperialism, is not a practicable solution. A world organization of sovereign states in which each relinquishes sovereignty irrevocably is a contradiction in terms; no sovereign state, even though it were to agree to be bound in many of its activities by international organization, would accept enforcement against it which destroyed interests it regards as important. The nuclear and other weapons of mass destruction have made the military potential of many individual nations quite equal to that of any international organization, rendering enforcement procedures impracticable. For behaviorist reasons enforcement would destroy the conditions required for a stable peaceful relationship. In any event there is no reason for believing that any form of international organization in a world comprising sovereign states would be acceptable as a decision-making and enforcement body.

Certain principles of national policy can be stated which, if followed, would lead to a condition of peace. It is assumed that governments would generally observe these once they had knowledge of them and of the consequences of their neglect. Nevertheless, knowledge and foresight cannot be assumed always to exist; and as a consequence, some conditioning of national policies is required in order to ensure that the principles of the theory of peace will be observed.

## 2. THE NATURE OF WORLD ORGANIZATION

The analysis has established that a condition of peace is a function of national policies, and not of external controls and enforcement. Reliance upon national policies for the creation of a condition of peace is the significant departure of this analysis from traditional approaches to international affairs. Traditional thinking and traditional policies have been concerned with the pursuit of immediate national interests by whatever means seemed expedient at the time, with their defense by force or by the threat of force, and with the forcible restraint of other nations with conflicting interests. Only in commercial relations after World War II was there a significant modification of this traditional all-against-all basis of policy. This traditional state of international relations rested on balances, alliances, and power bargaining. Our present analysis suggests, on the contrary, that a general condition of peaceful relations may be established only by determinate national policies.

Responsibility at the national level for the basic conditions required in a peaceful relationship is held to be fundamental; no form of external control could conceivably maintain peaceful relationships in modern conditions unless each nation were prepared to select those responses which induce passive reactions instead of those which provoke retaliatory ones. The need for some practical procedures on the international plane to ensure conformity with the principles of peace theory does not detract from the responsibility of individual nations. The back stop function of international controls cannot be effective except where there has arisen a mistaken perception, an error in judgment, or nontypical circumstances of discrimination or nonpassive adjustment. And it is not always effective here. Control could never be devised to maintain a condition of peace under all circumstances where each nation conducts its foreign policies without regard to the requirements of peace.

The unemployment analogy is useful once again. In a condition of general unemployment it would be impossible to deal with each unemployed person, either by means of repression or by job placement; but within the context of an inflationary policy the residue problem becomes manageable. A condition of peace is likewise a function of national policies. The residue problem, an important one it is true, is one which can be solved only if this national responsibility is observed. There cannot be any miraculous solutions to problems of international relations through the invention of ingenious international devices and organizations because if too great a burden is placed upon international organization, it will fail and expose a condition of deep hostilities. Control devices by themselves are no more than a backstop, a means of dealing with the exceptional.

Even in the treatment of the exceptional, however, the theoretical principles established must be observed. If the controls are not objective ones, if "undesirable" change or any failure to observe nondiscriminatory policies is dealt with by national and international restraints which provoke nonpassive responses, the condition of peace is destroyed. From a behaviorist point of view, justifiable control of undesirable change is just as likely to promote nonpassive responses and aggression as unjustifiable restraint upon desirable change.

In instances in which there is clear and universally accepted undesirability, the effects of world public opinion are probably as effective as any enforcement measures. The Suez dispute in 1956 was an example of this. If there is no overwhelmingly strong public sentiment, however, and if there is a clear division in thinking, the "undesirability" must be regarded as being subjectively related to the interests of a particular nation or group of nations. In this event any intervention would result in a conflict wider than that originally presented.

Although public opinion and the procedures of conciliation can be effective in resolving conflict, it is important that measures be found to prevent conflict from reaching an advanced stage where conciliation is required. This means that the environment must be conditioned by objective controls in such a way as to confine national *poli-*

*cies* within the limits imposed by the principles of non-discrimination and observance of the independence of nations, and by any other requirements which might be found necessary to a state of peace.

In practice this means the removal of the kind of enforcement procedures which traditionally have been regarded as imperative, and the establishment in the international environment of conditions which some Eastern philosophers assumed to exist when they postulated a condition of "natural harmony." It cannot be assumed that peace can be maintained only by a system of threatening forces, nor can it be assumed that there will be peace through the natural operation of human relations. It must be assumed that conditions have to be established which will control national policies, but without causing frustrations and nonpassive responses directed against any nation or group of nations.

In a sense this position is the meeting point of much Western and Eastern thinking. It requires first, the designation of those elements of national policy (such as non-discrimination and nonintervention) which consistently create—or avoid the destruction of—harmony among nations. And secondly, it requires the construction of an environment which will ensure that these national policies will be implemented. This nevertheless means still the introduction of the kind of enforcement which Western thinking has always assumed to be necessary before there could be the elimination of war.

By contrast, the significant difference in the present writer's position from that of both the East and the West is to be found in his belief that "enforcement" should be applied in advance to ensure the inclusion in national policy of those elements making for harmony, instead of to a particular situation already arisen in which disharmoney appears.

### 3. THE OBJECTIVE OF INTERNATIONAL ORGANIZATION

It follows that the objective of international organization should not be to provide an international police force, or in any way to create a central controlling legislature. The objective of international organization is properly a limited one. It should be merely to provide an organization through which understanding and agreement on a bilateral or multilateral basis may be reached. It should be to provide centers at which there can be discussion on a voluntary basis of matters of common interest among some or all nation states, including their disputes. It should be to provide a forum from which there can be a promotion of ideas and theories, the spread of knowledge regarding the basic principles of international peaceful conditions, and the advocacy of suitable national policies.

Examining the United Nations from this point of view there are discernible two fundamental defects. First, the United Nations, like the League of Nations, and like other proposals such as Kant's and many that were put forward even earlier, has rested upon enforcement. In the stated "Purposes and Principles" (Chapter One of the Charter) reference is made to the settlement of disputes on the basis of justice, to respect for territorial integrity, and to other related matters of national policy. The first purpose stated, however, and the one on which the structure of the organization was built, is "to take effective collective measures for the prevention and removal of threats to the peace, and for the suppression of acts of ag-

130

gression or other breaches of the peace . . ." (Article 1 of Chapter One.) Secondly, at no stage is there any reference to any principle of nondiscrimination in political relationships, or to the need for national policies conducive to a stable condition of peace. The Charter, indeed, does not reflect any concept of peace. The absence of war is to be brought about by "the settlement of disputes by peaceful means," and by collective action to suppress aggression, both of which presuppose as inevitable a state of circumstances in which there cannot be a condition of peace.

As long as it is assumed that enforcement is possible in international life, little attention is paid to national policies required by a condition of peace. If it is assumed, on the other hand, that international organization of sovereign states cannot exercise enforcement powers (in any circumstances, and especially in a nuclear world), then the pursuit by every state of national policies conducive to a condition of peace becomes the matter of most concern. In the first case, the purpose of organization is considered to be to make efficient its final powers over national states; and in the second, the main objective is to encourage, and by various devices to ensure, that national policies do conform to the requirements. The operations of the organization will be directed, in the second case, toward national policies, rather than toward situations in which conflict has already developed.

### 4. NEUTRALISM

We have already described the essentials of national policy which appear to be required if a condition of peace is to be created and maintained. Broadly, they hinge upon

131

nondiscriminatory responses to change, which also must have the characteristic of being objective in any restraints they might impose upon other nations. Translated into policy terms, national policies of this nature could be described as "neutral."

"Neutralism" used in this sense should be carefully distinguished from one conventional use of the term employed in the fifties to describe the policies of some independent Asian states, which were better described as "nonaligned." The "neutralism" of these states was in respect only to the conflict then prevailing between the Great Powers. India, for instance, discriminated against South Africa in political and commercial relations because of South African racial policies which affected her nationals there. It was the Indian Prime Minister who insisted upon the use of the term, "nonaligned," as being the term most appropriate to the policies of the countries formerly called the "neutrals." The two terms are likely to remain confused in popular thinking because policies of "neutralism" are required to be adopted by the main powers in relation to the underdeveloped countries, which happen to be the countries not aligned in relation to the dispute between the Great Powers.

Neutralism, however, has a more general application, particularly in dealings among the Great Powers. It can take many forms from nondiscriminatory commercial policies to nondiscrimination in political relations, including such questions as diplomatic representation, the entry of persons and publications, and the creation of neutral zones.

## 5. THE STRUCTURE AND PROCESSES OF INTERNATIONAL ORGANIZATION

Neutralism as the basis of the foreign policies of all nations is the theoretical objective of international organization, and we now turn to consider the structure and processes which would be appropriate to this objective. There are three basic characteristics of international organization which encourage neutralism and achieve peaceful international relations:

(a) Organization must be *associative*. Any international organization is self-defeating unless it is wholly associative, that is, unless it tends to bring nations together into an international community. In Chapter Two it was observed that the United Nations has tended to be dissociative in that it has spread and broadened conflict by making local dispute a matter of rivalry among Great Powers. It has also sanctioned exclusive military alliances, which are dissociative. There are at the same time associative factors in operation, even in a situation of conflict, as when there is integration through conflict. International organization must be so constructed as to take the fullest advantage of these associative factors.

(b) Organization must be *decentralized*. A highly centralized organization suffers from a tremendous administrative burden; and furthermore, it cannot be an informed and efficient agency for the creation of conditions of peace and the settlement of disputes. A central body could, it is true, have a useful research and consultative function, but it is unlikely to make an effective contribution even so to the speedy settlement of local disputes.

(c) Organization must rest upon the work of *specialized agencies*. As far as possible, international co-operation should be on a technical and not on a political basis; the breakup of international relations into their detailed operations—for instance, commercial relations, navigation, and health—tends to remove step by step a large proportion of day-by-day transactions from the arena of possible political dispute. They are handled on a *specialized* or technical basis, without publicity for the most part, and in an atmosphere in which fact and sensible compromise can become the basis for agreement.

Decentralization and specialization in international relations are known respectively as *regionalism* and *functionalism*. Regionalism[1] is a form of international organization limited in membership, but with functions and objectives which may be unlimited. Functionalism, on the other hand, designates a form of international organization which may be universal, but which is limited as to function and to purpose. For instance, the Economic and Social Council of the United Nations has had several regional organizations, and it has also had associated with it a number of specialized or functional agencies.

Regionalism, strictly speaking, would seem to refer to international organization on a geographical basis, and this is its normal usage. As such, however, the term has a limited application and may be misleading. Geographical proximity may be the greatest single factor in the evolution of subsystems; but the reason for this is not proximity *per se* so much as language, cultural, economic, defense, and other ties which tend to bind peoples together within

---

[1] See Lerche, C. O.: *Principles of International Politics* (New York: Oxford University Press; 1956). Morgenthau, Hans J. and Thompson, Kenneth W., eds.: *Principles and Problems of International Politics: Selected Readings* (New York: Alfred A. Knopf; 1951), and Strausz-Hupé, R. and Possony, S. T.: *International Relations* (New York: McGraw-Hill Book Co.; 1950).

a region. Exploration, conquest, and trade carry these ties to points outside the original geographic regions, lessening the importance of mere proximity as an integrative factor. An example of strictly geographical regionalism was the Pan American Union, or Organization of American States, established in 1948. However, this association was no more integrated than, and was little different in kind from, that of the British Commonwealth, members of which were scattered throughout the world. In between these two extremes there have been a number of organizations usually described as "regional"; but the geographical influences were not the most important. SEATO included nations outside the region, but not all those within it. The Arab League was within a region, but more importantly, it had a linguistic and cultural basis. The Communist countries have geographical propinquity, but this is secondary to an ideological basis of association. It is appropriate, therefore, for the term "regionalism" to connote all forms of association among limited numbers of nations, whether the association has developed out of strictly geographical circumstances, or out of common linguistic, cultural, traditional, ideological, and other features which tend to bind nations together.

Both regionalism and functionalism may be either associative or dissociative.[2] The 1953 proposals for a political union of six Western states could be regarded as integrative or associative; they were intended to draw the six nations together without at the same time increasing barriers to co-operation with nations outside the group, or

[2] See for discussion of associative trends, Mathisen, Trygve: *Methodology in the Study of International Relations* (Oslo: Oslo University Press; 1959).

provoking their hostile and retaliatory responses. The British Commonwealth could not be regarded as dissociative once Imperial Preference was no longer a feature. The Pan-American Union, the Arab League, and the Afro-Asian community have had strong associative features, but also some dissociative ones. NATO, SEATO, AN-ZAS, and the Warsaw Pact, on the other hand, being exclusive military alliances directed against some outside groups of powers, were strongly dissociative regional arrangements.

Specialized organizations dealing with Civil Aviation (ICAO), Education (UNESCO), Health (WHO), Postal Services (UPU), Telecommunications (ITU), and others of this nature are nondiscriminatory, universal, and integrative functional arrangements. The operation of sugar, steel, and oil combines, which seek to control markets in the interests of particular nations, are predominantly dissociative. There have been a number of private organizations (some of which were formally registered with the United Nations), such as the International Chamber of Commerce, the International Federation of Christian Trade Unions, and others which could have no universal application; and these have probably tended to be dissociative.

### 6. REGIONALISM

The progressive development of regional organizations of the type contemplated in Chapter VIII of the United Nations Charter (even though the military arrangements assumed to be sanctioned by Article 51 were still to remain in existence) could help to solve some pressing problems of international organization. Chapter VIII of the Charter implies, as we have already argued (see Chapter Four), that all nations, regardless of their power-bloc affiliations, should be members of the regional group. It also implies that conflict should be resolved within these organizations. Furthermore, the Security Council has been obliged to rely upon these regional organizations for the settlement of disputes. Chapter VIII provides, in effect, a plan for decentralization of international organization.

Decentralization helps directly to prevent the development of conflict situations, and assists in the settlement of disputes. First, the various regions of the world tend toward a cultural homogeneity within themselves. The countries of Africa, Europe, and South East Asia, for example, comprise groupings which have faced common problems, and which have had many common experiences. Debate, discussion, procedures, and negotiations are likely to be more fruitful in these circumstances. The New Delhi Conference of 1949 on Indonesia comprising Asian, African, and Middle East governments, was a regional meeting in the sense that those attending had common policies in respect of independence, and all had experienced subjection. Being interested in issues of independence, they were all well informed on Indonesian affairs and quickly arrived at an informed and responsible recommendation to the Security Council which contributed to a final settlement.

The discussion of local conflict situations within a regional group tends to confine the issues to those immediately relevant, and to exclude strategic and other considerations of interest only to outside powers. If the Congo situation of 1960-1 had in the first instance been dealt with by an established regional organization of independent African states, less opportunity would have been given to the Great Powers to pursue their conflicting interests in relation to Africa, and in relation also to the central organization of the United Nations.

Conflict integration is given greatest scope in regionalism. Clearly some measure of integration is likely to take place in a conflict situation by virtue of the very fact that conflict implies, at least in the earlier stages, some contact between the parties. But there is more involved than mere contact. The first step in any integration, as with compromise, is to uncover the conflict. When the demands of both sides are broken up, then it is possible for the parties to evaluate the issues. This is far more likely to take place in a regional discussion than at a centralized forum comprising one hundred nations.

At the present stage of development of political science, it is not necessary to argue either for the advantages of decentralization in administration or for the benefits of conflict integration. The first problem which requires solution is to determine what form and structure would best incorporate these advantages.

After World War II there was in the economic field a high degree of decentralization under the central direction of the Economic and Social Council. This decentralization took two forms, first in the creation of a number of specialized agencies, Food and Agriculture, Health, UNESCO, UNICEF, and others, and secondly, in regional organizations such as the Asian and Far Eastern, the European, the African, and the Latin American regional organizations of the Council. It would be difficult to estimate the associative influence of this vast network of economic organization. The sessions of the Economic and Social Council and of the specialized agencies were not news—they had few administrative problems with sufficient political implications to justify headlines. There were inefficiencies and arguments about contributions and priorities; but the work of the agencies and of the regional bodies was smooth, and the sessions of the Council placed no undue burden on the central administration. Indeed, if it were not for this associative work, the United Nations would probably not have commanded much popular support even in the majority of countries which took a special interest in the United Nations.

Two questions arise. First, why was this decentralization of the Economic and Social Council possible, and why was there no similar development in the Security Council? Secondly, and a related question, are the conditions which militated against decentralization in the political field still operative?

Postwar reconstruction planning commenced on an international basis even before the end of hostilities, and in the context of prewar analyses of the causes of war, which were economic in emphasis. By the time the Charter conference was convened at San Francisco in 1945, there was in existence a number of specialized agencies, and it was a matter for easy agreement that they should be brought into relationship with the United Nations. The Council had, therefore, a co-ordinating function from the outset. The development of regional consultation on economic matters was, from a political and practical point of view, an easy operation welcomed by all governments despite political differences. On the political side, there was no such body of agreement and no organization to be incorporated into the United Nations. Chapter VIII of the Charter merely provided for the future development of political regional organization. There was no organ responsible for initiating this development, and there was no world public opinion which saw its need. The Security Council was conceived as a body with the negative function of stopping conflict, unlike the Economic and Social Council, which had the positive function of creating conditions in which conflict would not arise. In 1945 it was not appreciated that ideology and political rivalry could, quite apart from economic conditions, create conditions of hostility, and nowhere in the Charter was provision made for the study of fundamental political problems in international relations. Furthermore, the distrust and suspicion among the Great Powers of the prewar and wartime periods continued, and a certain degree of informal military alliance existed among them. If the Security Council inherited any decentralized political organization, it was of this dissociative type, which finally took the form of military pacts. These added to the burden of the Council and did nothing to relieve it of its responsibilities in respect of the resolution of conflict.

It is interesting to note that at San Francisco the Latin American States pressed hard for the recognition of regional organizations, pointing to the achievements of the inter-American system. Supported by the United States, they managed to have the present Article 51 inserted into the Charter. However, the agreement which constituted the Organization of American States made three years later was not inconsistent with Chapter VIII. The intention was the regional settlement of disputes and the general co-operation envisaged in Chapter VIII. There were regional defense objectives also, but none which would not reasonably fall within the purposes of Chapter VIII. Unfortunately, and probably because they were never consulted over the Dumbarton Oak draft, the Latin

Americans failed to grasp the opportunity of giving the United Nations a model for Chapter VIII, and they provided, by introducing Article 51, the justification for regional military pacts which were at that stage not intended by any delegation.[3] Has the world environment changed in any way which would make possible even now the developments intended under Chapter VIII?

There have been since 1945 a great many developments conducive to associative trends. No estimate of the practical significance of any is possible; all that can be said is that they are in practice associative and to this extent helpful to regionalism and integration. The possession by the Great Powers of nuclear devices has altered the political situation and in some respects assisted in resolving conflict. East and West seem now to be more inclined to accept nonaligned governments and compromise solutions in areas of undetermined political allegiance. An extension of nonalignment and even of neutralism to the most troublesome of political situations, Germany and Korea, is in the nuclear age at least conceivable. Neutral zones provide many prospects of increased areas of agreement which would condition both the environment and the national policies of the main power rivals. In 1960 the Great Powers, together with other interested countries, agreed to a neutral zone in the Antarctic. Article I states: "Antarctica shall be used for peaceful purposes only." Article VII provides for observers to ensure the carrying out of the agreement. Article IX provides for a meeting of the parties to work out any problems which might arise. If the principle of

[3] See McDermott, W. C., ed.: *Documents on Inter-American Co-operation* (Philadelphia: University of Pennsylvania Press; 1955), Vols. I & II.

neutrality is accepted by the Great Powers as a device by which their competition might be controlled, there is no reason why other neutral zones should not be created. Once there is an acceptance by the Great Powers of neutralism as a possible means of avoiding nuclear conflict, the way is open for the resolution of conflict on a regional basis, on the basis of local facts and circumstances, and without reference to Great-Power rivalries.

There have been, as has already been pointed out (see Chapter Three), very great sociological and political changes in the two main rival systems. The virtual end of colonialism, the development of the welfare state in the West, the acceptance by the West of communism as a system, the ideological and practical changes which have emerged in the Communist states, their recognition of the viability of capitalism, together with the common fear of nuclear warfare, seemed by the end of the fifties to be leading to an international political environment in which compromise and integration would be possible.

There were other environmental changes which tended to make possible regional integration. For instance, before World War II, with unemployment and competition from low-cost countries a constant fear, each nation was defensive in its policies, and regionalism where it did exist was dissociative. The British Commonwealth's maintenance of Imperial Preference is an example. After the Great Depression and World War II there was confidence in the ability of financial policy to maintain high levels of employment. There was an accepted stability in the domestic economies of the advanced countries. Associative trends were strengthened as a result. Advanced industrial countries which had discriminated against low-cost producers were able to import large quantities of Japanese goods with the minimum of political reaction. Integration of developed and underdeveloped countries, even customs unions and joint developmental planning, could be contemplated.

The independence of states is in itself an associative factor. Colonial areas were usually administered in the interests of the metropolitan power, and underdeveloped states in the same region so administered had little opportunity for co-operation. Independence removed this dissociative factor, making possible the closer association, or even unification, of neighboring states previously under separate colonial control. And there have been in addition many other associative trends, including improved communications and education, which help to create an environment less favorable to dissociative regionalism and more conducive to integration and regional co-operation in political relations. But assuming that the environment is, or is likely to be, ripe for regionalism in political relations, what form is possible?

There were regional arrangements which were essentially associative in the period after World War II. The British Commonwealth, the Pan-American Union, and the Afro-Asian community, were strongly associative. The Arab group and the Communist countries both had important regional functions in relation to the settlement of disputes. The British Commonwealth in particular, after 1960 when its membership contained many nations of different stages of development and of different cultures, had an important associative influence in the world community. These were organizations outside the United Nations; but they made a contribution to the objectives of the United Nations and thus relieved it of some of its burden insofar as they avoided dissociative policies and actions.

Most nations were within some group of this character. However, regional arrangements of this kind touch only the fringe of the problem of conflict, for it is not within these groups that conflict is most likely to arise. Formal regional arrangements of the kind implied in Chapter VIII must be superimposed on these more natural associations in order to reduce their dissociative features and to encourage associative activities among members of different groups.

Regional groups of small powers are possible, and in a sense the Afro-Asian community constituted one. There would be some advantages in the formation of regional groups which excluded all Great Powers, so that regional disputes could be resolved in their absence. This would also solve difficulties which would occur whenever a region happened to contain opposing Great Powers. It would avoid the danger of nations' being dominated in a regional organization by any one Great Power. However, in order to obtain the maximum benefit of integration through conflict, and the maximum influence of small powers on world affairs, strictly geographical regions would seem to be necessary. This would mean that the Great Powers would be represented only in those regions in which they had their metropolitan territories and would have no claim to interests outside their own region. This is a reversal of traditional procedures; even ECAFE included all Great Powers. It is, however, a procedure more in accord with a world structure of independent nations, and more likely to result in peaceful settlement of local disputes. The pattern of international political relations which would develop would be, say, six regional organizations, Europe (including Russia), Asia, Oceania, Africa, the Levant, and America, each a little United Nations in itself. The main function of the central organization would be to hear reports from these local organizations, to deal with issues referred to it, and to refer issues for advice. Among the disputes which could not be dealt with by this simple system of decentralization would be those arising between countries in two different regional organizations, and disputes over territories controlled by a power not in the region. The central administration would have, in these cases, the additional function of arranging for consultation between regional organizations.

The objective of regionalism coincides with the objective of international organization, which is to promote neutralism in national policies. The particular application of regionalism will vary according to the circumstances prevailing. As has been stated, the competition between the Great Powers in the nuclear era has been most acute in the underdeveloped areas. It is the nonaligned countries, and countries which are aligned only as a result of economic and political pressures, that are likely to be the casualties of ideological conflict. It is over their allegiance that Great-Power conflict and open warfare are most likely to occur. The introduction of objective controls in this competition is important to these countries, and also to the development in world politics of an approximation to a condition of peace.

It has been observed that the nonaligned countries do not form a bloc. They tend to work together only on those matters relating to independence, on which they have common views. Even after the Bandung Conference of 1955 no formal continuing organization was established. The consultations among Asian countries which took place at New York during the fifties did not represent any form of alliance and were not backed by any formal administrative arrangements. The nonaligned nations do not form a third power. Nevertheless, the common interest of the countries of Asia, South East Asia, Africa, and Latin America in obtaining and maintaining practical independence affords opportunities for imposing controls upon the militarily and economically strong powers, controls which the latter would have no choice but passively to accept. For instance, it would be in the interests of the nonaligned nations to agree to receive economic assistance and technical aid only through an established international organization which would be guided by considerations only of need and of availability. Agreement among them to limit arms, to institute their own inspection teams, and to submit disputes in the first instance to their own regional organization would be consistent with their nonalignment policies.

Agreement between "neutrals" to restrict the diplomatic and attached representation of the Great Powers, and to rely more upon the United Nations as a center of diplomatic activity and upon United Nations agencies for assistance and advice, would lessen competition for their allegiance and help to ensure their nonalignment. The pressures which underdeveloped countries experience can be measured in terms of foreign establishments which operate within their territories. It is not unusual for Great-Power missions in the capitals of small powers to number more than one hundred. Diplomatic procedures other than those that appear in handbooks, including the financing and influencing of political parties and individuals, are known to be widespread. From time to time independent states endeavor to limit the size of foreign missions and to control their activities; but acting alone, such states could prejudice an important source of assistance and economic aid without achieving the immediate objective. To place responsibility for the control of Great-Power competition on small, underdeveloped countries is unrealistic. Until newly created states develop the institutions and powers of the modern state, they cannot possibly withstand the propaganda and calculated subversion of competing power blocs.

There is one device by which pressure may be reduced, and that is for the nonaligned countries to confine their diplomatic and consular representation to the United Nations center, and to seek the extension of United Nations services so that its agencies throughout the world can be empowered to carry out diplomatic and consular functions on behalf of member nations. This would not only curb the activities of Great Powers, but it would also ensure that small nations are represented in foreign countries by skilled, trained, and denationalized public servants.

For reasons of cost, if no other, it is surprising that a procedure of this kind has not been adopted. Postwar diplomacy has, from an administrative point of view, become farcical. Great-Power diplomatic missions in small countries, grandly housed and numbering hundreds, including messengers and door keepers brought from home, cannot possibly be justified in terms of national interest, of information collected, or of improved relations. Prestige and Parkinson's Law alone are satisfied. When smaller powers consider that their status demands reciprocal engagement in the game of universal diplomatic representation, the cost becomes out of all proportion to any possible national gain. In any event, while missions provide opportunities for dissociative activities and rivalries, they add little to the conduct of international relations. In modern conditions of immediate communication, no representative to another country is permitted freedom to do more than routine speech making, social entertainment, and consular duties, without reference to his government. The reporting function is of limited value, as better informed and more experienced observers are usually to be found outside diplomatic missions, in which staffs change frequently. And in any event diplomats are not always encouraged to report unwelcome facts.

These are merely examples of the devices which can be introduced to curb competition; some may be relevant in one circumstance, some in others. The need is for a constant search for objective controls that can make a useful contribution to the environment in which major powers operate. As Mr. Nehru wisely observed: "It is not a question of believing the other party's word: it is a question of creating conditions where the other party cannot break its word, or where it finds it difficult to break its word." [4]

### 7. FUNCTIONALISM

Functionalism can have a similarly integrative effect and could also take some of the burden from the United Nations. Indeed, it is already doing this. Agreements which were operative even before the creation of the United Nations, covering navigation, post and telegraph, health controls, and a host of other matters, have since World War

[4] Indian Parliamentary Debates (Delhi: Sept. 29, 1954).

II had many others of far-reaching importance added to their number.

We tend to take these for granted. International conferences take place concerning them, and amendments and extensions are agreed to; but they receive little or no publicity. They come to a political level for formal reasons; they are mostly negotiated on an official level. Indeed, many of them are so much a part of the recognized code of behavior that continued formal agreement is not always required.

It would be a mistake, however, to regard these agreements or controls as being of no significance merely because they are taken for granted. They were not at one time so regarded. It is a general human habit to accept the existing situation and to overestimate the difficulties which stand in the way of innovation and development, and the time they take to formalize. The fact is that new rules are being introduced continually; and additions during the period following World War II were remarkable.

### i: Commercial Agencies

Some of the Rules of General Agreement on Tariffs and Trade deserve special notice in the light of the prewar history of discrimination and trade blocs. Article I incorporates the most-favored-nation clause in its unconditional and unrestricted form. This clause is the cornerstone of nondiscrimination in international commercial relations. Article VI is concerned with anti-dumping and countervailing duties. Article XIII sets out to control nondiscriminatory administration of quantitative restrictions —to apply the principle of most-favored-nation treatment to the administration of quantitative restrictions. Under Articles VII, XII, and XXIII a contracting party aggrieved by the imposition of restrictions by another party may resort to consultation with the country concerned, or it may appeal to the Contracting Parties for joint action. Retaliatory action is not permissible. There are nullification provisions in Article XXIII which provide some guarantee against possible malpractices. As one commentator has observed:

> The fact that all the contracting parties unanimously found it necessary to strengthen and enlarge the Agreement and to place it on a permanent basis with a well-defined organization of its own, is the best proof of its practical value and its great service. Undoubtedly G.A.T.T. represents the most outstanding achievement in the field of international trade and commerce. Great hope can be placed on the flexibility of the Agreement, and the singular evolutionary tendency hitherto manifested.[5]

International economic conferences, at which important decisions are made each year, have become, like post and telegraph meetings, so routine that in many cases representation by officials and not by political leaders is sufficient for drafting an agreement.

One reason for this may be that Russia has not a great deal of interest in Western trading problems. The importance of full employment in the main consuming areas to the economic activity of other areas is something which Russia recognizes but regards as a matter to be argued between countries within the capitalist bloc. So also with tariff and many other trading discussions. This is not to say, however, that Russian co-operation has been absent.

[5] Seyid Muhammad, U. A.: *The Legal Framework of World Trade* (London: Stevens and Sons, Ltd.; 1958), p. 316.

Communist countries, even though they have no contractual obligations, have found it expedient to arrange their procedures and policies in order to conform with the established pattern of trade. Most-favored-nation treatment is a characteristic of Soviet trade agreements. This is an inevitable consequence of the G.A.T.T. provisions which provide that in bilateral agreements with nonmember countries the test is whether the agreement causes injury to members. Even before the G.A.T.T. formal provisions, the United Kingdom and Russia agreed in a treaty of 1930 to be guided "in regard to the purchase and sale of goods . . . by commercial and financial considerations only."

### ii: Economic Assistance

Operations handled by specialized agencies have been singularly effective. They have given the least possible opportunities for political dispute, and have by their operation done much to ease political tension by reason of the contacts established. Operations which have not been placed in the hands of specialized agencies, however, have encountered political difficulties. This was so in the case of economic aid and technical assistance. UNRRA (the United Nations Relief and Rehabilitation Administration) was established in 1943. Its indiscriminate aid was an international force of gathering momentum. In 1946, however, the revolutionaries were challenging the status quo —Russia was injecting propaganda into international relations and challenging Western leadership. Aid and technical assistance were then seen by the West as political weapons. In 1947 both the United States and the United Kingdom decided to withdraw from UNRRA, which made funds available to regimes in Communist-controlled countries. Early in 1948 the United States Congress passed the Economic Co-operation Act, in which were stated methods and conditions of aid. Subsequent aid arrangements in Europe and in Asia were discriminatory, and politically and strategically oriented. They were a part of the cold-war tactics.

The fallacy in Great-Power thinking regarding aid lay in the association of allegiance with a type of economic and political society. There is no reason to believe that a Communist-controlled country cannot have friendlier relations with some capitalist country than with some other Communist countries. Planned systems and the appropriate political institutions were introduced into underdeveloped countries through necessity, and the withdrawal of aid would not remove this necessity. Nor would the supply of aid, unless on a scale impossible to contemplate. There is undoubtedly a strong tendency for like to be associated with like in international relations; but it is a tendency only, and one strongly enforced by policies which assume it to be overriding. If an Asian country, today friendly toward the West because of traditional ties, adopted a Communist system, there is no reason why friendly relations should not continue, provided of course that the West did not oppose the change and did not act on the assumption that relations would change. If the objective of aid is to create conditions which satisfy the requirements of peace, that is to say, acceptable minimum living standards and rates of development, then prevailing political systems should be irrelevant.

In the ideological struggle of the sixties, competition for the allegiance of underdeveloped countries has been one of the most likely causes of political and military conflict. Discriminatory aid was but one weapon. For this reason aid has not been organized through a specialized agency and on a nondiscriminatory basis. With greater acceptance of neutralism, however, and a greater desire on the part of the main powers to avoid conflict in these areas, functional organization might be applied in this field also. Certainly, if either of the main powers were to agree to operate only through a nondiscriminatory specialized agency, it would be difficult for the other not to cooperate. The recipients, mostly nonaligned countries, would clearly prefer this arrangement.

Economic and technical aid is an operation which could best be carried out by a functional agency. It is a highly specialized technical operation; it is not just a matter of sending surpluses that might be available to whatever country might appear to want them most. Aid is no longer a missionary endeavor. To be effective in its objectives, it requires specialist attention and planning, with careful field analysis of each circumstance. It is an operation which cannot easily be accomplished by any one nation acting alone.

Even though channeled through a functional organization, the competition in aid between Great Powers could nevertheless be very great if the allegiance of the recipients were still considered to be an important goal. While the United States is in a better position in terms of capacity to make aid available, it is by no means certain that capacity is the main factor. In some respects those countries which appear best able to afford—in terms of living standards—aid contributions on a large scale are least able to contribute. Galbraith has argued this point at some length:

153

As a society becomes increasingly affluent, wants are increasingly created by the process by which they are satisfied . . . Wants come to depend on output. . . . We do, each year, provide some aid to others. But first we have a prayerful discussion of whether or not we can afford the sacrifice. The question is, indeed, inescapable, since production keeps wants abreast of itself. . . . In recent times no problem has been more puzzling to thoughtful people than why, in a troubled world, we make such poor use of our affluence. . . . Now it is clear that the trouble lies much deeper.

He notes also that the existence of technical problems will not be regarded as an excuse:

Elsewhere in the world, it is our vast well-being and not the urgency of our need which is evident. The nineteenth-century plutocrat who devoted his energies to expanding his already considerable income . . . who came to the aid of the poor only after a careful consideration of his ability to spare from his needs and the realistic likelihood of revolt and disorder if he abstained . . . was not in all respects an attractive figure. Thus with nations.[6]

The international organization of economic and technical assistance, together with the acceptance of neutralism, would tend to remove from competition and rivalry that aspect of international relations which holds the greatest threat of limited war. The stage would be set for intensive but peaceful economic and political competition for the allegiance of nonaligned governments.

[6] *The Affluent Society* (London: Hamish Hamilton; and Boston: Houghton Mifflin; 1958), Ch. 10.

### iii: *Political Functionalism*

Functionalism has not penetrated far into international political life where it is most needed. Functions carried out by political bodies such as the Security Council, and which have a significant technical content, are better delegated to specialized agencies once the main political decisions are taken. Any disputes which might arise are then dealt with on a technical basis and not argued by the Security Council, or on the propaganda platform of the Assembly. For instance, once agreement in principle is reached on a nuclear-test ban, the control of export of arms, the control of intelligence agencies, or some other matter of political content, a specialized agency is best able to implement the agreement. The close, continuous, and usually friendly contact between specialist members of the agency, and their own personal interest in the success of its work, create a background of co-operation not likely to be achieved in a body such as the Security Council, whose members are continually changing and in any event are more concerned with diplomatic victory.

When the time comes that functionalism achieves a breakthrough into political fields, there are a number of operations which are likely to be undertaken. For instance, the transition from dependence or trusteeship to independence presents in some cases a problem leading to conflict. Peoples demand for themselves, and other nations tend to demand for them, independence before there is sufficient experience and sufficient political stability. The intervention of the United Nations through the Security Council into the affairs of an independent state tends to become a source of Great-Power rivalry, with the interests of the dependent state being of secondary concern. A specialized agency created to give administrative assistance and advice, and if necessary to assume responsibility for law and order, with no more political supervision than is given to other specialized agencies dealing with monetary or health matters, would relieve all powers of the political responsibilities they frequently find it embarrassing to exercise.

Even the Security-Council function of the peaceful settlement of disputes could be assisted by a selected body of specialists concerned in particular with resolving conflict, and studying continually the requirements of peaceful international relations. A Security-Council secretariat well equipped to advise and to make recommendations to members is one form such a specialist body could take. Although most functional organizations rely heavily upon the skilled staff of their secretariats, in the case of the Security Council no such development has taken place. It is at this point that there could be a spread of responsibility as demanded by the Soviet in 1960.

*iv: Research*

One means of breakthrough is by the organization of research into political and sociological relationships by a formal international organization. Haas observed:

Clearly, the efficacy of international organization does not derive from any powers analogous to those of national governments. It [rests instead on] the need felt by national groups and elites for the services commonly performed by assemblies and secretariats. If the research is judged impartial and useful, its findings may see application. If the advice rendered by technical assistance missions is such as to meet the interests and values of local groups, it will usually be accepted. The long-run, unspectacular impact of international organizations, therefore, is to be found in the research and advice function of the agencies.[7]

The United Nations structure includes the Assembly, the Security Council, and the Economic and Social Council, which have many specialized agencies some of which are concerned with far-reaching investigations and proposals. The Security Council, the political body under the Assembly, and the Economic and Social Council, the economic body, cannot be regarded as similar in function. One is the political trouble shooter, and the other the long-term economic trouble avoider. There is no long-term *political* trouble avoider. There is no point within the Secretariat or within the organization as a whole at which fundamental political studies can be carried out. The nearest approach is probably the personal staff of the Secretary-General; and if he were to extend his activities in this direction, all kinds of complaints would be made, according to the inquiries being undertaken and their findings.

Nonnational studies are left to national academic institutions. This has many disadvantages. First, nationals cannot divorce themselves from the national environment. The same person working in an international or nonnational environment would start with different attitudes and end with different conclusions. Secondly, the work of Great-Power nationals swamps the work of all others. This is not necessarily because it is academically better,

[7] Haas, E.B. and Whiting, A.S.: *Dynamics of International Relations* (New York: McGraw-Hill Book Co.; 1956), p. 440.

or because Great-Power nationals have a monopoly of wisdom. It is merely because Great Powers have facilities and populations which make possible the publication and distribution of the work of their nationals. Most writings today on international relations are American. There is throughout Asia a constant flow of studies and ideas which, if published and distributed as is American material, could make a positive contribution to the solving of some of our pressing political problems. Thirdly, a national working in a national institution is confined to a large degree in his studies and source materials available to him, and in his language or languages. It is the out-of-the-way, the untranslated document, which is often most significant. An international research center would overcome some of these problems. The existence of research groups, the publication of international research, and its debate in an appropriate international organ would help to limit power-bloc rivalries and policies.

Among the studies which are needed at an international level are those connected with a condition of peace. For instance, the process of national adjustment is a much neglected but important study. We know that many adjustments are easier in a planned than in a free-enterprise economy. We know that in the latter, economic adjustment is easier in times of full employment and prosperity than in times of recession. There are but few examples of government intervention into the free working of the private enterprise system designed to facilitate adjustment to changes in market conditions; usually governments intervene by providing some sort of subsidy or protection to make adjustment unnecessary. The study of change and the adjustment to it, and of the effects on international relations of the absence of adjustment, is one which is relevant to a thorough study of the conditions of peace and of policies likely to secure peace.

The continued maintenance of a condition of peace requires that adjustments be made smoothly to every change, economic and political, as the change takes place. As a consequence, it is basic to a condition of peace that there should be close consultation among nations on changing conditions, with a view to ensuring that adjustments are within the capacity of the nations affected. In a sense this principle is accepted in international relations. International agreements against dumping are an application of it. The introduction of the full-employment obligation into the United Nations Charter is at least a recognition of the interdependence of nations on economic relations. After World War II there was a considerable development in consultation among all nations, regardless of their political organizations, on all matters of common economic interest. Many international agreements were entered into aiming at the prevention of national policies which could prejudice the interests of other nations. It should not be impossible to extend this principle so that through some suitable organization all nations would receive notice of possible change, and an opportunity would be given to make known the affected interests.

Indeed, some such organ within the United Nations would assist in the solution of a problem faced by all international organizations. In 1960 the Communist bloc at the United Nations charged the Secretariat with lack of objectivity, and made suggestions to ensure the adequate and equitable representation of the views of the Great Powers and of the neutrals. A research organization within the United Nations, broadly based in terms of national representation, could help to solve such a problem. The Secretary-General would have difficulty opposing recommendations made unanimously by national specialists; but he could be excused for using his judgment in cases where agreement does not seem possible.

## 8. THE WITHERING AWAY OF WORLD ORGANIZATION

A world organization with foundations resting upon a developed regionalism and upon an ever extending functionalism could become an effective instrument for international co-ordination of policy. The withering away of most of its central functions and the building up of these two integrative systems could provide a stable foundation for peaceful international relations.

Progress in this direction calls for an extension of areas of agreement, using regionalism and functionalism as the means. Instead of attempting to deal with the major areas of disagreement, as is usually the case in international negotiation, the aim should be to develop progressively a framework of agreement within which mistakes arising out of fallible judgment of long-term interest would be of limited consequence. There are already many controls imposed by the international environment which do not arise out of international agreement. They are, for instance, the geographical, meteorological, demographical, and anthropological factors within which national policies must operate. They include current resource development in the various parts of the world, economic differences in living standards, cultural differences in living standards, and cultural differences as they affect national organization and international relations. They are wholly objective in their operation. There are also rules, that is to say, those international agreements which are specific, *ad hoc*, and functional, which are reliably observed. Furthermore, there are restraints, those conditions which exercise from time to time an effective influence on policies and which, like "controls," must be accepted by policy makers as part of the environment in which policy operates, but which arise out of historic, cultural, and even psychological realities.

Clearly, the ideal world government is a body of controls and rules which effectively determine the total of international policies and the total behavior of each nation. In other words, the function of international organization is to assist in extending "controls," in so far as this is possible, and to add to the "rules" until the field of "restraints" is made precise and determinate.

What is here suggested is no more than was intended in 1945. The Charter of the United Nations contained the provisions necessary for the evolution of a decentralized United Nations. An unfortunate turn was taken as a result of cold-war circumstances. Now that the nuclear stalemate is forcing reconsideration of their policies by all the larger powers, the time may be ripe for the objectives originally intended.

### 9. DOMESTIC ADJUSTMENTS

A condition of peace is a function of national policies. National foreign policies reflect domestic policies and problems. It is likely that until changes take place in the internal policies and institutions of all powers, a condition of peace cannot be established. It is certain that in the continued ideological conflict that will take place in the absence of military conflict, the nation which can adjust itself most readily to the changing requirements of international society is the state most likely to win the support and allegiance of its own people and of the peoples of the underdeveloped countries.

We have already noted the changes which have taken place both in free-enterprise and in controlled economies during the first half of the twentieth century. By the fifties the need for even more substantial change was at least recognized. The weaknesses of national structures which have an international bearing are many and varied. The West has problems peculiar to itself. It has unemployed resources, including manpower, and wastes of competition which in a world of want cause antagonisms. It has discriminatory policies based on color; it has very great inequalities, and poverty in the midst of plenty. It has an unused capacity which its own peoples, and peoples elsewhere, need. In periods of relative prosperity this causes internal and external resentment. In periods of recession, or of competition with growing economies such as the Communist economies, unused capacity could lead to domestic political situations requiring further protective devices, with increased international tension. Equally in the political field, barriers to adjustment, pressures to ensure political conformity, and prejudiced attitudes toward new forms of government are current in periods of prosperity. In critical periods of economic recession, increased protection against the competition of hostile ideologies would be advocated as a means to economic stability.

The problem of adjustment in the Western type of economy is not an easy one.

Our achievements cannot conceal the fact that there are many shortcomings in this country. . . . We have problems of race relations, aliens, intolerance.

. . . It is essential that our domestic affairs be so ordered as to give the world a picture of a free, tolerant, progressive society which practices what it recommends. Thucydides quotes Pericles as saying: "For I am more afraid of our own mistakes than of the enemy's designs." [8]

George Kennan stressed this point in words which bear repetition:

The fact is that we in the West are, of course, engaged in a competition with Russia; but it is not the kind of competition the Russians claim it is. We are not pursuing the same objectives. We are not at the same stage of development; our tasks are scarcely similar. The real competition is rather to see who moves most rapidly and successfully to the solution of his own peculiar problems and to the fulfilment of his own specific ideals.

To my own countrymen who have often asked me where best to apply the hand to counter the Soviet threat, I have accordingly had to reply: to our American failings—to the things we are ashamed of in our own eyes: to the racial problem, to the conditions in our big cities, to the education and environment of our young people, to the growing gap between specialized knowledge and popular understanding.[9]

Newly developed democracies of the Western type have an even greater task of adjustment. Unemployment or

[8] Roberts, H.L.: *Russia and America: Dangers and Prospects*. Published for the Council on Foreign Relations (New York: Harper & Bros.; 1956), p. xxviii.

[9] Kennan, George: *Russia, the Atom and the West* (New York: Oxford University Press; 1958), pp. 13-14.

underemployment in a country of low living standards is a disease for which there are no technical excuses. The causes are constitutional or system based. It is here that the challenge to the status quo is greatest, in fact, irresistible unless quick and effective adjustments can be made.

Western countries give evidence of having made intensive examination of the Communist systems; attempts are made to attribute motives and to explain policies. Communist leaders, however, seem not to be briefed on the slow, exasperating, fumbling, unled procedures of decision which operate in a parliamentary system of the British type, which frequently are accompanied by provocative statements and opinions bearing no relationship to the final decision. It would be a terrible tragedy if the mere lack of understanding of procedures and of the time element in a free-enterprise system were to lead to actions which, with more understanding, would not have been justified. The forcing of issues, the cutting of the time factor, have been accomplished in the history of every modern nation by revolution. In terms of human gains and losses, the procedures could probably be regarded as justified by the results. In the current international situation, however, now that the nature of warfare has altered, losses must dwarf gains. Hence the importance of research, the examination of the other party's problems, and the evolving of politically practical solutions.

Communist countries are not without their own peculiar problems. These cannot be described by a Western writer; but they need nevertheless to be described. The conservative Communist reaction to change and resistance to adaptation is no less dangerous than were the conservative reactions of the West during the last century. Radical thinking in Communist countries is as necessary as in any other type of society in order that there can be constant adjustment to change.

Although both communism and capitalism have in the past shown themselves capable of doing the things which are presently needed, the H-bomb has been an obstacle to their doing so. Behind the H-bomb are accumulating adjustments which should be made, which normally promote a military clash, and which are ultimately made in the course of, and as a result of, a clash. The dialectic processes must now take place by some means which excludes force. This means that adaptation and adjustment, the requirements of competition in which war is excluded, must be forced by objective circumstances, by conditions which promote passive responses.

Historically, Western processes are attuned to the kind of imperatives introduced by the H-bomb; Western processes are attuned to progressive change and adaptation. Adjustment in thinking is required primarily in the Marxist camp, and it is a fundamental and difficult adjustment for Marxists to make. It is difficult particularly for the Communist leaders. Previously they were confident of early victory by processes which they understood and in which they had faith. Now they are forced to enter into a far more difficult process of interaction.

The present analysis suggests that in the absence of war the struggle between S and R will be won by that side which can the more readily gear itself to competitive conditions. Any resort to force can be interpreted as anticipated loss in this competition. It is, therefore, in the interests of both parties to ensure that neither is losing.

# 8

## Science or Judgment?

We have argued that a condition of peace cannot be brought about by international forces, nor by the domination of any national or international forces. It is, rather, a function of national policies. It can be brought about only by the pursuit of policies which invite passive response, and by national adjustments to changing conditions.

There are specific influences which condition national policy. There are, on the one hand, certain environmental controls about which the nation can do nothing; and on the other, there are certain rules which nations observe as a simple matter of expediency, as well as restraints imposed by consideration of expediency, world opinion, and the acceptance of principle. The state is, however, free to disregard rules and restraints, and its arbitrary decisions in these respects may ultimately create or destroy a condition of peace.

It can be assumed that the intention of each nation

state is to advance its national interests to the maximum. In a dynamic world in which there are constant changes, errors of judgment are likely to be made in the pursuit of self-interest. The judgment of expediency is a balancing of particular actions in terms of national advantage and disadvantage. In this process, the weight given to each involves a subjective estimate reflecting the history, education, politics, and psychological state of the one who does the balancing; and his interpretation of the political environment of the time cannot fail to influence his judgment.

A prejudiced nation's reluctance immediately to retaliate, and its inability to make a passive response, may hide the extent of faulty judgment. Even an accumulation of nonpassive responses may not be apparent, especially in circumstances in which retaliation is inhibited by military threat or power-bloc arrangements. It is only later that frustration and aggression appear. Some additional provocation, small in comparison with previous ones, is likely to touch off a reaction seemingly out of all proportion to the final stimulus. A critical international situation is likely to appear without any apparent relation to a particular event. National policies are then dictated by short-term strategic interest. A cumulative process of deterioration in international relations follows.

Objective guides and automatic controls are required to ensure against error in policy, and against self-destructive responses. The errors are errors of judgment. In every case of response, judgment has to be exercised. Foreign policy is based on no more than a small degree of enlightened self-interest, a subjective determination of national interest, and some humanism and good will. Every decision, no matter how trivial, is a political decision, that is to say, a decision based on the weighing of estimated advantage and estimated disadvantage in the light of prevailing circumstances. Negotiations between officials are without any objective criterion either for a condition of peace or for long-term national advantage. Such negotiations can only pinpoint, therefore, the differences on which decision has to be made at a political level. In negotiations of this kind the only guides are national strategy, national prestige, and immediate national economic or political gain.

Complicated machines, flying long distances and at great heights, require for their operation judgments beyond human capacity; only instruments can give accurate landing and airspeeds, and descent angles in relation to speed, levels, and height. Even after the 'judgment" is made by instruments, automatic execution of adjustments is desirable. In foreign policy, it is quite literally beyond human capacity to ascertain all the relevant facts and to make judgments which will produce reliably the results required. Between policy aims and policy achievements there is a widening gap. It reaches infinity when policy aims produce results which are the opposite of their objectives, as happened so often in the fifties when politically backward regimes were used as a defense against communism. Whether the issue be one of recognition, colonialism, or discriminatory aid, no government can anticipate all the unknowns, including the reactions of others, and be sure that the objectives sought will be the ones produced. There may appear to be all kinds of risks attached to following somewhat blindly a policy based on a theory; but the risks of following policies of expediency are far greater. In the real world, policies based on theoretical principles and modified according to considerations of pressing expediency are likely to achieve objectives more accurately than policies based on expediency and modified from time to time in deference to principle.

What is required in international relations is a yardstick, as there is in financial policy, a body of theory, a pattern against which national policy decisions can be judged. It is for this reason that we have in this work endeavored to describe a condition of peace and to formulate a theory. Clearly, the domestic policy and the foreign policy of each nation vary according to its national circumstances. We have been able to affirm, however, that regardless of all other considerations, the state in a condition of peace acts independently, and without discrimination in any form. It acts as a neutral with respect to the rest of the world. It is nondiscriminatory, not merely in relation to some particular power conflict, but in all its relations. The objective of national policy, according to our argument, is to move toward independence of national action in the pursuit of national interests and on a basis of complete nondiscrimination. This is the yardstick. This is the pattern of the peaceful orientation of national policy.

There is thus a distinction between policy based on theoretical principle, and that based on the subjective judgments of expediency. The distinction is between those policies which are in theory oriented to peace, and those which serve to satisfy some immediate domestic or foreign purpose despite possible damage to a condition of peace. It may appear expedient, electorally, to smear a foreign power and to run the risk of heightening international tensions. It may appear expedient in terms of strategy to bolster up unpopular governments and to run the risk of internal revolt and of inviting foreign assistance.

It may appear to be expedient to vote at the United Nations in a bloc, even though not agreeing with the measure under notice, and to run the risk of inconsistency in policy. All such acts of expediency could ultimately damage national interests. Unless the yardstick is an obvious, well designed, popularly visible one, very great mistakes affecting the national interest are likely to be made. The conflict between expediency and science is the conflict between the attractions of immediate gain as against a long-term advantage. It is, in human and political terms, the conflict between the relative attraction of a specific and currently obtainable gain, and a less specific and less certain but greater advantage later. An acceptable yardstick, and a recognized procedure toward a condition of peace, would predetermine a large proportion, if not a major proportion, of national policy. Foreign policy would be removed to a far greater degree than is presently the case from the field of controversy and of political expediency.

However, even the invention of a yardstick, and a political decision to use it, would not in themselves solve the problems of national policy. Fact, analysis, and insight are required even to evolve current policies based on theoretical principle. This has long been recognized in relation to economic policy. National economic policies are a compromise between very different and sometimes conflicting objectives. Economic policy based on theory must be tempered to allow for the pursuit of objectives which to some extent destroy the greatest possible division of labor. It is a specialist in economics who is employed to work out how best to achieve a noneconomic aim. There can be no absolute application of principles of policy; but knowledge of the theory makes possible its modifications

without destroying it. It is not for the defense expert, nor
for the development expert, nor for the colonial expert, to
make the judgment on the extent to which national policy can flout the findings of a condition of peace.

The development and application of a theory are a task
for the specialist. Yet in no nation is there a separation
of function between the pursuit specifically of peaceful
relations and the more general conduct of international
affairs, despite the fact that the great bulk of day-by-day
diplomacy has nothing whatever to do with peace and frequently involves policies which are antithetical to it. A
foreign department's formal function is to improve international relations, in the sense of promoting peace; but
it is also responsible for the co-ordination of the policies
of other departments of government. Most departments
of governments, on the other hand, are concerned with
some aspects of international relations. A treasury has
wide interests in the trading and financial field, and departments dealing with commerce, shipping, and publicity all have an interest in the whole field of international
relations. They are engaged in day-by-day negotiations,
and each has day-by-day special objectives and policies to
pursue. Defense departments, economic departments, and
all others expect to use for their own special purposes the
foreign department, whose job it is to promote peace. In
theory, of course, the foreign department should regard
it as its function to co-ordinate the economic and defense
departments from the point of view of peace promotion.
If it did this, it would be concerned with the development
of techniques and theories of peace, just as treasuries are
concerned with techniques and theories about the maintenance of economic stability. This theoretical ideal is, in
practice, impossible. In some circumstances the defense

171

and security authorities would regard policy recommendations with this end in view as damaging to their own policies. Equally, economic departments would not tolerate co-ordination which in the interests of peace sacrificed some important domestic interest.

Foreign offices try to handle the whole realm of international relations, and with as much success as those engaged in the study of international relations at universities. Just as there is in the academic world no *discipline* related to peace, there are no *policies* related to peace being developed by foreign offices. There are defense policies, economic policies, and others which, it might be argued, contribute to peace at a particular time by imposing restraints on a probable enemy; but these do not seek the establishment of conditions required to ensure peaceful relations over a long term. A separate department is required, concerned with peaceful relations. It would compete with other policy departments, such as defense and commerce, for influence on the co-ordinator—that is, the department of foreign affairs. Its duty would be to make recommendations as to how its objects could be attained alongside other policy objectives, and to make comments on the effects of other policies on the attainment of its own objectives.

The political environment is probably the controlling factor in making final decisions. In the absence of domestic and international crises, policies based on fact and principle are more easily pursued; but once internal political crisis occurs, political expediency dominates. Ironically, it is on these occasions that the following of fact and of theoretic principle becomes most important. A separate department concerned with conditions of peace would greatly assist in offsetting temptations to adopt political expediency, and in promoting policies based on objective fact and principle.

In a situation of crisis, in which the winning of a struggle is the objective, the strategy of each side is to exploit the weaknesses of the other. Thus in the fifties the West sought to weaken Communist political institutions, and the Communist governments sought to aggravate the problems faced by the West in underdeveloped regions. Once the struggle ended in stalemate, with the constant danger of thermonuclear warfare, a new pattern began to emerge. Once the objective of policy is not to win a victory over an enemy, but to secure a position in which the "enemy" will be adopting policies consistent with a condition of peace, the appropriate policies will be to refrain from exploiting disadvantages, and to assist in overcoming those of each other's weaknesses which gave rise to aggressive motivations.

Such reversals of thinking do not, of course, take place by conscious thought processes at a political level; but they do take place. The academic studies of Keynes demonstrated that an expansion of credit was the appropriate policy in periods of depression, whereas previously governments tended to reduce expenditure. It could be that foreign policies currently pursued tend to defeat their peaceful objectives, and herein lies the importance of specialist studies in international relations.

The inadequacy of this analysis is all too apparent. What has, it is hoped, been demonstrated, is the possibility of, and the need for, a new pattern of thinking, a theory of peace, and a practical guide to policy—the substitution of science for prejudiced judgment in the pursuit of peaceful international relations.

# 9

## The
## Point of Responsibility

The rethinking of policies, the evolving of a theory, the dissemination of findings, the formulation of practical policies, and the acceptance of these policies are procedures which take many years. In the meantime there is constant danger of deliberate or of accidental war.

It is relevant for the political scientist interested in peace theory to examine the political environment in which he works, and to contemplate the practical ways in which there can be a translation of theory into practice. His exposition should be directed not merely to scientists, but to lay people and to political leaders as well. Which of these is of most immediate concern is a relevant matter for inquiry.

## 1. PUBLIC OPINION IN THE MODERN STATE

People in various parts of the world want and demand the abolition of weapons of mass destruction and of war itself. Yet there is no evidence that the probability of global war is an important issue of popular concern; and there is day-by-day evidence that where popular demand does exist, it is not effective. There are two interrelated reasons: first, the politically underdeveloped state of public opinion, and secondly, the dictatorial nature of government and the influence of weapons of mass communication.

War has been through the ages a recognized instrument of national policy, an instrument with which generation after generation has learned to live. It is one with which are associated the highest national honors. Church and state have throughout history justified it, supported it, and celebrated it; and this condition still persists in the West. War is part of modern culture. The human casualties of war have been far fewer than those inflicted by disease, and more recently, by travel. Despite warnings by scientists, sometimes deliberately offset by political statements circulated through the mass media, there is far more popular interest (though still very little) in wiping out disease and in preventing deaths on the highway, than in preventing war.

Popular attitudes were not altered by the invention of weapons of mass destruction. Those who rely upon the deterrent effects of modern weapons fail to see that the threat of mass destruction does not alter the mental processes of choice by the individual.

175

This greatly increased destructiveness is said by some to have altered radically the cost-gain ratio in warfare, to have made war exorbitantly unprofitable, and hence to have eliminated war as a rational instrument of national policy. Such a conclusion . . . rests on the dubious premise that wars have been started as the outcome of cost-risk calculations. . . . We cannot assume that the advent of the atomic bomb or thermonuclear bomb has fundamentally altered the conditions causing conflict between nations. The possibility remains of a collective decision to accept death rather than real or imagined servitude, dishonor or loss of status.[1]

The last war is an instance of this, when men took up arms despite the belief throughout Europe and England that gas would be used and would bring mass death. In Britain the fear of annihilation gave rise to far less political activity than did the delays of the government in coming to grips with Nazi aggression. That gas was not used, probably the result of technical difficulties, in no way invalidates the conclusion that both leaders and people were prepared to risk mass death rather than be defeated by Hitler. The threat of mass destruction does not alter the human attitude. Indeed, the modern community, West as well as East, bears such overwhelming allegiance to its leaders and is so powerfully influenced by the mass media that any government or leader in a modern state prepared to wage righteous and defensive war is assured in advance of widespread support, regardless of risks.

Moreover, there is no evidence of any great public in-

[1] Roberts, H.L.: *Russia and America: Dangers and Prospects* (New York: Harper & Bros.; 1956).

terest in the particular issues at stake in international conflict. Ideology has been the dominant feature of the present world crisis. The conflict has been depicted in clear-
cut terms: communism *versus* the Free World. Yet it
cannot be said that there is widespread concern about
issues of freedom in Western countries. The threat to
academic freedom, to industrial freedom, and to freedom
of public expression, arising out of the activities of security services; the threat to individuality arising out of
the means of mass communication in the hands of a few,
and out of social pressures to conform politically; all may
be regarded by articulate minorities as matters of the
gravest concern. They leave unaffected, however, the great
majority of people in the most advanced countries. These
freedoms are not being exercised by the great majority
of people and are therefore of little concern to them. This
is even more the case in the underdeveloped Communist
countries in which the majority of people are now enjoy-
ing a reasonable living standard which is new to them;
they would assuredly not experience concern about the
lack of freedom of a minority of intellectuals and others
who may wish to oppose Communist policy. Ultimately
the issues at stake are made to appear only as a clear
choice: slavery or death, annihilation or surrender, or
some such alternative, deliberately simplified.

It is not soil, climate, or racial traits that induce people
in one area of the world to support one ideology, and similar people elsewhere to support another; it is a large measure of indifference to the conditions of life outside food,
clothing, shelter, and entertainment—an indifference ex-
ploited by newspapers, radio, school and religious education, and official propaganda. The indifference of people
generally in all countries to issues which a minority holds

important is usually greatly underestimated by that minority. The view propagated by the modern state that security steps are necessary, and the image of the enemy implanted by the modern state in justification of its own policies, are universally accepted except by small minorities within each state. These minorities usually have freedom to doubt; but there are many restraints placed upon them and methods of discreditation levelled against them if they seek to provide effective leadership against the conventional wisdom of the governing forces.

This is not an overdrawn picture of the modern state. Whether Communist or capitalist, freedom is something exercised within limits imposed by the state, and these limits are such that there cannot be any fundamental disagreements with the broad ideologies of those that govern. The qualification, "modern" state, is important; for a loosely organized state is far less secure, and indifference and resignation can, under leadership and by circumstances, be turned into desperation and action. It is the usual experience of newly developed and politically backward nations to have civil disturbances, revolts, and revolutionary changes.

C.Wright Mills is concerned with the American state, but his comments have a general application among modern states:

> The top of modern American society is increasingly unified, and often seems wilfully co-ordinated: at the top there has emerged an elite of power. The middle levels are a drifting set of stalemated, balancing forces: the middle does not link the bottom with the top. The bottom of this society is politically fragmented, and even as a passive fact, increasingly pow-

erless: at the bottom there is emerging a mass society. . . . The American elite does not have any real
image of peace—other than as an uneasy interlude
existing precariously by virtue of the balance of
mutual terror. The only seriously accepted plan of
"peace" is the fully loaded pistol. In short, war or a
high state of war preparedness is felt to be the
normal and seemingly permanent condition of the
United States.[2]

During the Cold War of the fifties there was a development of powerful intelligence organizations whose view
it was that in a democracy politicians must be protected
from judgments influenced by public opinion, by sentiment, by argument and discussion, and by negotiations.
In this view, continuity in policy and the long-term security of the state cannot be left to political judgment
altered by circumstances and pressures. Intelligence organizations act in the belief that they have the facts and
are best in a position to make a judgment of national
interest, and that political obligations rest therefore upon
them. In their view this is not a denial of "democracy"
or of parliamentary control; it is just a fact of reality, a
necessary part of a system in the modern world where
there are other states in which the decisions of politicians
are less colored by irrelevant political considerations.
Furthermore, they believe that they are not acting against
the interests of the state or in any "treacherous" or "sub-
versive" way when they consult with, and co-operate with,
similar organizations in other friendly countries, to control the policies of the governments under which they

[2] Mills, C. Wright: *The Power Elite*. A Galaxy Book (New York: Oxford
University Press; 1959), pp. 324, 184.

serve. They would, however, regard any similar efforts by civilians as being inimical to the state; and indeed, similar acts by civilians are treason in the eyes of the law. In short, there is in the modern state, in addition to the pressures of the power elite through the mass media, the operation of part of the military organization to hold the government to certain policies in the event of undue influence by outbursts of public opinion, or by the leadership of other elites, or by the misdirection of mass media, or by the compromises which might arise out of international negotiation. These are, as it were, the final safeguard which protects the state against the situation in which inadequate mass media and an insufficiently sophisticated power elite might fail to prevent changes in policy considered dangerous by the self-appointed trustees of national security.

John Kenneth Galbraith contributes a view which seems to modify to some degree the concept of the "power elite" of C.Wright Mills, and to credit public opinion with more influence. He makes use of the concept of "conventional wisdom." He seems to imply that conventional wisdom, expressed by the political or social leader, is in fact the wisdom of the mass, ascertained as a result of public relations activities. Respectability and familiarity are important features of "conventional wisdom," and clearly political leaders attempt to identify themselves with it. But whether political decision reflects conventional wisdom of this order is open to serious doubt. On the contrary, the conventional wisdom in the field of foreign and defense policy is the wisdom of political leaders, applied frequently despite the beliefs of a majority of members of the community.

Galbraith recognizes certain difficulties in his concept

when applied to military policies, and rather confirms the view of Mills. The conditions which Mills describes as applying to all fields of government probably applied much earlier to military policy.

> On few matters does the conventional wisdom have such authority as in military policy and international affairs. The problems here are difficult and infinite in their ramifications. Old ideas and old formulas are rocks on which men can stand. They are cherished as much as new thought, which so adds to the complexity of an already uncertain and complex world, is resisted. Moreover, where military policy is concerned, the effect of peace is to exempt the conventional wisdom from any test of experience. Since, as noted, it is ordinarily only experience which exposes error, the conventional wisdom is here admirably protected. Countries have rarely gone to war, at least in the last century, without discovering that the military wisdom which they had treasured in the previous period of peace as the nearest thing to divine revelation, was, when put to the test of circumstance, remarkably foolish.[3]

He then quotes many examples of wrong judgment, any one of which could be regarded as crucial in terms of military strategy.

The difference is a matter of importance at least to those political scientists whose work is designed to evolve procedures by which established fact will enter into policy making. If current policies of modern states are based

[3] Galbraith, John Kenneth: *The Affluent Society* (London: Hamish Hamilton; 1958), p. 128, and (Boston: Houghton Mifflin; 1958) pp. 163-4.

on conventional wisdom, as Galbraith describes it, then the long-term procedure must be to educate and to change popular thinking before events demonstrate in fatal fashion that this wisdom is at fault. If on the other hand current policies are based on the viewpoint of power elites, and especially the military power elite, the long-term procedure is to evolve policies which take this viewpoint as one of the relevant facts in any test of political practicability, and to formulate theory and policy in terms which show that their objectives can be achieved without war.

If we modify Mills's view to the extent of including within his concept of the power elite the effects of conventional and traditional thinking and the influence of public opinion on matters with which it is *en masse* familiar, and Galbraith's concept to include the concept of a power elite contributing to conventional thinking and capable of defying it, an approach to reality emerges.

On either view, however, it is clear that in the modern state, Communist or capitalist, "public opinion" cannot be relied upon as a significant factor in directing policies along a long-term course toward a condition of peace, or in preventing all-out warfare. There may be devices by which public opinion can be reinstated. This is a matter for the political scientist to consider. It would seem, however, that a progressive reduction in the effectiveness of public opinion can be expected, especially in relation to questions concerning international affairs and security. It has to be assumed, therefore, that the power elite and the military ethic are part of the environment. These are the realistic facts which follow from the realistic fact of sovereign states. This is the context in which academic studies have to be made.

## 2. LEADERSHIP IN THE MODERN STATE

The question arises as to whether academic studies should be directed to political leadership on the assumption that the latter has the qualities necessary to recognize and to implement practical processes.

Both the power elite of Mills and the conventional wisdom of Galbraith exist; the conventional wisdom is the wisdom of the power elite. Sometimes in knowledge and in insight this wisdom drags behind the views of informed minorities. This would not be generally apparent. The power elite is protected by all the advantages to be derived from conventional wisdom. It has attributed to it prestige, respectability, insight, and even infallibility. The fact that it is proved wrong by events time and time again is of no great public significance. It is popularly believed to be all-wise and all-knowing, and it is thought to be backed by a powerful and skilled public administration.

The example of the foreign office is the appropriate one. Its typical operation demonstrates the point. A foreign minister and his foreign office are popularly regarded as the center of information about foreign affairs, a place where information is sifted, where objective judgment is arrived at. Consequently, the official statements made and the policies followed are popularly considered to be those which wisdom suggests are the best means to preserve peace. The true situation is quite otherwise.

A foreign office is the administrative medium through which government policy is carried out. It naturally must work within the limits set by national and governmental attitudes and philosophies. This applies as much to the recommendation as to the execution of governmental decision. It is not a responsibility of the foreign office to undertake fundamental studies as part of its official work. It would not be regarded as appropriate, for instance, to examine the grievances of potential enemies from the latter's point of view, nor to try to ascertain fundamental causes of tension. No Western foreign office made objective studies before the last war of the political effects on Japan of Western tariff policy. It is not the function of a foreign office to challenge the basic assumptions of national policy, nor to question basic attitudes and philosophies. In any event, recommendations and the studies on which they are based will always be made from the point of view of national interest and advantage. This is the function of a foreign office. Its purpose is to preserve the status and to safeguard the interests of the nation and its government.

Having in mind the practical pressures imposed on a foreign office by other departments of government, and by the current policies and attitudes of the government of the day, it must be assumed that officers of the foreign office will tend to report from overseas, and to select information available from various sources, in such a way as to make a contribution to the formation of politically feasible policies. The only facts and opinions regarded as relevant will be those which fall within the framework of broad government policy, and which are compatible with the basic assumptions on which government policy is conceived. There will be "reliable" sources, those which support government policy, and "suspect" sources, which have the unfriendly habit of producing facts which do not support government policy. Very important human factors, of course, creep into activities of this nature. The desire for promotion, the need not to offend by producing embarrassing facts, the reluctance to report from overseas events which would suggest policy was wrongly based, are all most relevant influences in the final formulation of a national policy. Thus it is that a foreign office can be wholly ill informed about events in a country in which it is strongly represented. This was, it appears, the position of the United States State Department prior to the success of the Communist revolution in China.

The basis of foreign policies is reflected in this administrative pattern. The pattern itself reflects implied assumptions that a condition of peace is not possible, and that war can be prevented only by alliances and by strategic-diplomatic balances. The conventional wisdom, the respect, and the prestige which attach to a foreign office, in the belief that the foreign office is primarily concerned with the maintenance of a condition of peace, are fraudulently acquired; the conventional wisdom which justifiably could be attached to a foreign office is that relevant to a department of defense.

The device of "secrecy" is the one in which foreign and defense departments take refuge. The purpose of secrecy is not primarily to prevent a potential enemy from learning strategic plans or policies to be employed in circumstances anticipated. It is rather to protect leadership from public scrutiny of its mistakes, its political expediency, its convenient disregard for fact and advice, its disagreements with allies, and its "horse trading" with other powers. There is probably no more powerful device employed by the modern state than that of secrecy. It destroys the purpose of certain democratic institutions, such as the "question-time" of the Parliament, the legal processes by which citizens have protection against wrongful punishment, the public examination of policy, etc. Indeed, it destroys opportunities for the academic examina-

185

tion of policy and problems, for the facts are not made available to the public.

Yet it is not necessary to assume that the motives of the power elite are sinister. The conduct of the elite, including secrecy, is not something inherent in the nature of the elite or inevitable in terms of human organization. Basically the problem of the power elite is lack of knowledge, lack of information, lack of education and experience. With all the goodwill in the world, and given the dissemination of all the knowledge existing today, international relations would still be much the same as they are. Clearly there can be no general understanding either of the nature of the problems occurring in international relations, or of their solution, until the subject matter is systematized and related to a body of well known and internationally accepted propositions.

This places a great responsibility on the scientist. He may put forward what appear to be sensible proposals; but once he gets close to the political mind, to the person who is working from the traditional assumption of basic conflict of interest, he realizes how unreal are his proposals. He realizes that there are so many committed men— Chinese, Russian, American, French, British, who adhere to their own points of view despite opportunities for human communication, for fear of loss of their own standing or self-respect, or merely through an inability to comprehend—that objective study and recommendation could be a futile waste of time. Even on matters of far less concern and seemingly far less controversial, such as domestic economic policy, a studied exposition prepared for the politician, deliberately phrased in his language, is apparently incomprehensible or so foreign to his thinking in the environment of political expediency that it cannot be used.

This is one of the relevant factors which the scientist must take into account. It is part of his problem. Expositions have to be attuned to the ears of policy makers. This is not to say that only those policies with which politicians are familiar should be advanced; the policies which analysis demands, and no other, must be put forward. But they must be put forward in terms which are comprehensible and applicable to policy making. The solutions themselves have to ring true in terms of local experience and environment, and the problems currently being experienced.

Looking back over the postwar period, on the one hand, at the policies of governments and the problems they face, and on the other, at the work that has been done in the field of international relations, one is aware that the scientist has made a disappointing contribution. He has made all kinds of suggestions regarding current political policies of disengagement and disarmament, but very little contribution to the solution and exposition of some of the more fundamental questions which are a prerequisite to disengagement and disarmament. The more outstanding contributions of Kennan and others who have succeeded in detaching themselves to a commendable degree from the environment in which they live have, after all, made a contribution to national strategy rather than to international peace.

The studies which may ultimately prove of most value are those more philosophic and speculative ones with insight based on the kind of detailed study which makes possible observations of great simplicity, observations which little by little make possible an understanding of the social, economic, and political environment in which the problems of war and peace must be solved. Insight and observation of this order are required in relation to current political problems. We have to be able to discard all preconceived notions about the enemy, all assumptions on which we and our governments have been working, all propaganda influences and habits of thought, and to start again. These comments apply with as much force to Communist writers as to those of the West. It is high time the former challenged their own assumptions that the policies of their governments are historically infallible. Even if we were to assume this to be true, until Communist writers can convince the West by reason and analysis, the problem of conflict remains. It will be of little satisfaction to anyone, if all-out war comes, to say: "But our policies were right!"

Before disputing parties can come together and usefully ask each other what the strife is about and what agreements are to be made, an analysis of conflict has to be made on an academic plane with all the objectivity of science. The initial responsibility devolves upon the scientist in the field of peace theory, and no useful progress on a political level can be expected until theories are formulated, made public, and widely accepted.

# 10

## On the Study and Teaching of Peace Theory

A theory of peace opens up many new fields of inquiry. The important aspects of the study of international relations are not international organization, deterrents, resource distribution, balance of power, and the many other matters which frequently are included in conventional studies of the subject. The important ones in the nuclear era are aspects not as yet investigated: the nature of responses, the processes of adjustment, and behaviorist studies not previously thought to be of concern to the student of international relations. Reconsideration of the study and teaching of international relations has probably to precede the reconsideration of structures and institutions no longer relevant. Some comments on the study of the subject seem appropriate in this final chapter.

It is not intended here to traverse the controversies which have taken place regarding the content of international relations and the possibilities of developing a precise course of study. The present intention is merely to point out the implications of the foregoing analysis—especially in relation to the development of a separate study of a condition of peace—for the teaching of international relations.

The traditional approach to the study and teaching of this subject stems from Western political thinking, which has assumed the need for certain balances and international devices for the prevention of warfare. The subject matter has been concerned primarily with power rivalries and their control. As a background, studies have been made of national economic and political conditions. Morgenthau and Thompson in *Principles and Problems of International Politics* made a selection of subject matter:

> In determining what is relevant to our subject matter we have . . . started with the assumption . . . that the core of international relations is international politics and that the subject matter of international politics is the struggle for power among sovereign nations.[1]

Kirk regards the field as comprising the following:

> International law, international organization, and international politics. . . . In summary, the study of

[1] Morgenthau, H. and Thompson, K., eds.: *Principles and Problems of International Politics: Selected Readings* (New York: Alfred A. Knopf; 1951), Preface.

international politics centres around an analysis of national power, an understanding of the means by which international relations are conducted, and conflicts of interest adjusted, and an evaluation of the philosophical, legal and moral bases, not merely of the present state of world development, but those of the emerging world society.[2]

The term "international relations" has been widely used to describe all aspects of relations between countries and peoples, peaceful and otherwise: legal, cultural, economic, geographic. Professor Sprout of the United States has reported that "international relations" in his country is employed "to designate all human behavior that originates on one side of a national boundary, and affects human behavior on the other side of the boundary." Professor Chevallier of France refers to a *complexe*, meaning all facts, whether or not related to peace, which enter into the realm of international relations.[3]

An examination of the courses of study at leading universities reflects this same approach. A useful survey is contained in an International Studies Conference publication, "The University Teaching of International Relations." [4] While courses vary greatly, they mostly comprise some history of international relations, the development of law, international organization, and studies of contemporary problems. In the United States in particular, area

[2] Kirk, Grayson: *The Study of International Relations in American Colleges and Universities* (Council of Foreign Relations Publication; 1947), p. 14.
[3] Manning, C.A.W., ed.: "The University Teaching of Social Sciences—International Relations," UNESCO Report (UNESCO: Feb., 1954), p. 10.
[4] Edited by George L. Goodwin. (Windsor: International Studies Conference; 1950).

studies are characteristic. These require intensive language courses so that original source material can be used.[5] Nowhere in the surveys made can one find reference to the study of theory. The need for some theory is recognized; Manning, for example, does not believe that the further accumulation of facts is as important as insights into international relations.

In the late fifties studies were concerned with functional relationships, which we have described in the foregoing analysis as extended areas of agreement. Several writers were impressed with the degree of international integration which was developing by reason of the negotiation and operation of many functional agreements.[6] The basic assumption of inevitable conflict, however, remained. The American national studies, and in particular those dealing intensively with probable enemies, led more directly to studies of war and of military tactics than of international relations.

Huntington summarized this trend in the study of international relations:

> The postwar decade saw a startling change in the prevailing academic approach to international relations. In the 1930's the emphasis had been almost entirely upon the question of form and structure studied in courses in international law and international organization. The basic value premise was usually the desirability of world organization. By the late 1940's, however, American writers were vying with each other in denouncing the moralism, legal-

---

[5] See Columbia University Bulletin, "The School of International Affairs."
[6] See Strausz-Hupé and Possony: *International Relations*; Lerche: *Principles of International Politics*; and Mathisen: *Methodology in the Study of International Relations*.

ism, utopianism, Wilsonism, and sentimentalism of American diplomatic past. "The statesman," Morgenthau warned, in contrast to earlier American view-points, "must think in terms of the national interest conceived as a power among powers." Another aspect of the academic change was the increasing attention given in colleges and universities to the problems of national security. Courses were established in foreign policy, military history, and defense policy, and institutes blossomed to further research in these areas.[7]

The objective of some of these studies was to ascertain "what strategic doctrine is most likely to enable us to avoid the dilemma of having to make a choice between all-out war and a gradual loss of positions, between Armageddon and defeat without war." [8] This realism thereby tended to exclude consideration of nonmilitary alternatives.

Some curious studies logically followed from such a concept of international relations.

The key problem of present-day strategy is to devise a spectrum of capabilities with which to resist Soviet challenges. These capabilities should enable us to confront the opponent with contingencies from which he can extricate himself only by all-out war, while deterring him from this step by a superior retaliatory capacity . . . the psychological advantage will always be on the side of the power which can

---

[7] Huntington, S.P.: *The Soldier and the State: The Theory of Politics of Civil-Military Relations* (Cambridge: Harvard University Press; 1957).
[8] Kissinger, H.A.: *Nuclear Weapons & Foreign Policy* (New York: Harper & Bros.; 1957), p. 136.

shift to its opponent the decision to initiate all-out war.[9]

Another writer in the fifties, Roberts, suggests a different solution:

> From our discussion of the potentialities of thermonuclear weapons and the nature of Soviet Communism we conclude that a general war, whether we won it or not, or the world-wide establishment of Communism, whether through general war or by other means, would each constitute a disaster of terrible magnitude. Yet we cannot simply make the avoidance of *both* war and Communist hegemony an absolute policy requirement, since avoiding the one might, under certain circumstances, mean accepting the other. If the choice is put in these narrow terms, the answer has to be that the United States must prevent the world-wide establishment of Communism —even at the cost of general war.[1]

These conclusions follow naturally from the assumptions which are implied in the approach to the subject. Opportunities for negotiation do not exist once it is assumed there can be no trust, that the probable enemy is inherently dishonest, and that all his peaceful proposals are merely tricks or tactics in playing for time. Even in theory, negotiation becomes irrelevant if it is assumed that "the Soviet bloc refuses to accept either the frame of the international order or the domestic structure of the non-Soviet states." [2] In this view "it is futile to seek

[9] Ibid., p. 144.
[1] Roberts, H.L.: *Russia and America: Dangers and Prospects* (New York: Harper & Bros.; 1956), p. 80.
[2] Kissinger: op. cit., pp. 95-6.

to deal with a revolutionary power by 'ordinary' diplomatic means." [3]

Whether a dictionary definition of international relations is taken, or the description contained in the handbooks of leading universities, or the actual studies currently made in a particular period, the general approach to the study has been traditionally in terms of international institutions, international politics, power rivalries, international strategy, and enforcement procedures.

Our analysis has been concerned with a condition of peace. Deterrents, balance of power, international enforcement, and other devices which are conspicuous in traditional studies of international relations, we have found to be incompatible with a condition of peace. They cannot, therefore, be regarded properly as part of the study of peaceful international relations. *Peaceful* international relations is a subject for study quite separately from other international studies. It is a specialized discipline in relation to which there can be developed a separate body of theory. Our analysis raises, therefore, important questions regarding the teaching and study of international relations generally, and in particular the study of peaceful relationships.

A study of all the world and the relationships between its parts is clearly beyond the ability of any one person. For this reason alone great difficulties must be experienced in the teaching of international relations, and in the development of a separate discipline. Manning discovered that there were in the world very few universities in which there was a separate study of international relations. He found that almost always international relations was a combination of various disciplines or parts of

[3] Ibid., pp. 317-37.

them: law, economics, political science, etc. Alternatively, to overcome the problem of scope, some universities have arranged for the "slanting" of the older disciplines so that a student could read law, economics, and other connected subjects from the point of view of his interests in international affairs. There has been in some cases an organization of interdepartmental committees—the "interdisciplinary" approach to the subject. Sometimes there have been attempts to use the study of international affairs as a means of bringing about an integration of learning.

Such devices may have helped in the teaching of particular aspects of the subject of international affairs; but none could make possible the total comprehension of such a wide field by either student or master. In these circumstances, the tendency has been for those working in this field to take some part of it which interests them, and to endeavor to build up procedures which might be regarded as making their study scientific. The selection of the field and the methods employed are a result of their own personal interests, background, and immediate experience. Studies may depend upon a subjective assessment of facts, not all of which are known, by people whose political philosophy and cultural background must inevitably color their judgment. The quite arbitrary selection of segments of the total field is, therefore, no substitute for a logical breaking down of the total field into studies similar in nature to those in the established disciplines of economics and political science.

It has been assumed that the unsystematized study of international relations was dealing broadly with the study of peaceful relationships. But as we have seen, the studies which purport to be studies relating to peace are in fact studies of political warfare, of military strategy, of international organization, of power balances, and of other enforcement devices. There has been no endeavor, so far as one can ascertain, to develop a study which would be concerned with peaceful relationships.

Once the term "international relations" is discarded and the far more limited study of peace is considered, there is a clarification of relationships between academic fields and between different parts of the *complexe*. The international aspects of political warfare, of defense strategy, of law (including the laws of war and the treatment of prisoners of war which are also part of the study of international relations), and the international aspects of psychology and anthropology, are all within the scope of each of the disciplines dealing with these subjects. The fact that they are international does not remove them from the main body of their relevant theory. Together they may form a *complexe*, but this describes a total human situation and is not a description of a study. There are undoubtedly those who will be interested in reading about some of the international aspects of some or all of these disciplines. But they will not necessarily be studying *peace*, which is indeed a separate study. It is as specialized and as limited as each of these other disciplines, and like them it is one in which the organization of facts and a body of theory should be possible. Assuming that the study of a condition of peace should be separate from studies of other aspects of international relations, we may seek to define its nature and scope.

We have already defined "peace" as a situation in which there is absorption of change, or nonaggressive but protective responses when absorption is not possible. This definition includes the maintenance of stable peaceful relations between states and peoples which have independent governments, not necessarily the same in form or in character; between states and peoples which have widely differing living standards and cultural development and wish to retain what gains they have made without sacrifice, even for peace; between states and peoples which have different views and philosophies; between states and peoples which wish to promote their own philosophies beyond their own boundaries. The study of peace, far from being unconcerned with the possibility that some people may be forced to make sacrifices in terms of their own independence, their individual beliefs, and their living standards for the sake of international peace, is, on the contrary, deeply concerned to discover ways and means of establishing peaceful international relations without destroying variations in national cultures and philosophies.

From such a study should be excluded all considerations which do not bring to bear upon the subject of peace. For example, *ad hoc* measures which might be advocated as a means of removing a particular tension or as a means of solving a particular political problem, are likely to be based on some currently held point of view which has no sound foundation in fact or in theory. There are those who advocate the limitation of arms in one form or another as a means of improving relations and of making possible further negotiation. There is, however, as we have already argued, no reason to believe that any disarmament is possible while tension exists, or that disarmament, if it were possible, would in fact lessen tension and lead to wider negotiations. In the same way the creation of international forces, regional defense agreements, the support of particular types of governments, and other *ad hoc* devices designed to deal with a particular situation may not in practice do other than further aggravate a situation, as did the ill-founded economic policy which restricted credit in times of recession. These do not form a part of the study of a condition of peace.

Defined in these terms, the study of peace is both wider and narrower than the traditional study of international relations. It does not include many kinds of subject matter which have occupied most attention in international relations. On the other hand, it does include areas which have traditionally not been regarded as part of the study of international relations. For instance, many behaviorist studies, sociological studies of the modern state which throw light on national responses, adjustment processes in various types of economic and political organization, and other matters affecting the ability of nations to register passive responses, are all relevant to a study of peaceful international relations.

Studies of this nature are not as yet available for undergraduate use; they are still exploratory. They will not be available until there is a body of theory which clearly indicates those areas which are and which are not relevant to the study of peace. The possibility of such a theory has already been asserted, and would provide a basis for the study of international peaceful relationships quite as surely as a theory of pure competition provides a basis for other economic studies. To attempt to understand international relations by means of area studies, or historic studies of power rivalries, or the operation of deterrent devices, is not likely to be more successful than an attempt to understand monopoly and oligopoly without first examining competition. Without some examination of a condition of peace, the nature and consequences of enforcement and the functions of international organization are likely to be erroneously conceived. The emphasis is likely to be on the prevention of warfare rather than on the resolution of conflict and the prevention of conflict situations. Area studies lead to a concentration on enemy motivations, instead of on the ability of the enemy to make adjustments. The concept of peace is unfortunately grounded in international terms, and not in the terms of national policies. Any consideration of policy is likely to emphasize defense against change, rather than adjustment to it.

If there were an acceptable basis of theory, undergraduate courses and graduate studies would take a direction quite different from the traditional. A history of the subject, including early philosophic thinking, and in particular the changes in thinking which occurred during the first half of the twentieth century, would be relevant. Behavioral responses, conflict integration, and related case studies would assume importance. International organization would be examined from a functional point of view relevant to the basic theory of a condition of peace, rather than from a structural point of view relevant to early beliefs regarding the standing of R in relation to S.

In only one instance have we been able to find an emphasis of this nature, and that is in Mathisen's study, *Methodology in the Study of International Relations*, which was published as recently as 1959.[4] While he reflects many traditional points of view which appear incompatible with his general approach, due recognition is nevertheless given to the importance of the changes taking place in the natural environment, "socio-cultural"

[4] Mathisen, Trygve: *Methodology in the Study of International Relations* (Oslo: Oslo University Press; 1959).

change, "associative and dissociative trends," the behavior of states, and other phenomena with which we
have been concerned. This work, together with sociological studies in the United States and a growing emphasis
on functional co-operation and behaviorist responses
which has in recent years been appearing in works on international relations, gives reason to believe that a new
approach to the study of the issues of peace is developing.

A NOTE ON THE TYPE

THIS BOOK is set in ELECTRA, a Linotype face designed by W. A. Dwiggins (1880-1956). This face cannot be classified as either modern or old-style. It is not based on any historical model, nor does it echo any particular period or style. It avoids the extreme contrasts between thick and thin elements that mark most modern faces, and attempts to give a feeling of fluidity, power, and speed.

*Composed, printed, and bound by*
*H. Wolff, New York.*
*Typography and binding design by*
VINCENT TORRE